OUTPERFORMING WALL STREET

Stock Market Profits through Patience and Discipline

Daniel Alan Seiver

Prentice-Hall, Inc., Englewood Cliffs, New Jersey 07632

Library of Congress Cataloging-in-Publication Data

SEIVER, DANIEL ALAN.
    Outperforming Wall Street.

    Bibliography: p.
    Includes index.
    1. Stocks—United States—Handbooks, manuals, etc.
I. Title.
HG4527.S395 1987   332.63'22   86-22541
ISBN 0-13-645219-1
ISBN 0-13-645235-3   [PBK]
ISBN 0-13-644931-X

Editorial/production supervision: *Denise Gannon*
Cover design: *Lundgren Graphics, Ltd.*
Manufacturing buyer: *Carol Bystrom*

The publisher offers discounts on this book when ordered
in bulk quantities. For more information, write:

Special Sales/College Marketing
Prentice-Hall, Inc.
College Technical and Reference Division
Englewood Cliffs, New Jersey 07632

Stock table shown as background to cover and chapter opening
pages copyright © 1986 by the New York Times Company.
Reprinted by permission.

Printed in the United States of America

10 9 8 7 6 5 4 3 2 1

ISBN   0-13-644931-X   025

PRENTICE-HALL INTERNATIONAL (UK) LIMITED, *London*
PRENTICE-HALL OF AUSTRALIA PTY. LIMITED, *Sydney*
PRENTICE-HALL CANADA INC., *Toronto*
PRENTICE-HALL HISPANOAMERICANA, S.A., *Mexico*
PRENTICE-HALL OF INDIA PRIVATE LIMITED, *New Delhi*
PRENTICE-HALL OF JAPAN, INC., *Tokyo*
PRENTICE-HALL OF SOUTHEAST ASIA PTE. LTD., *Singapore*
EDITORA PRENTICE-HALL DO BRASIL, LTDA., *Rio de Janeiro*

To RTS—just for kicks

CONTENTS

PREFACE

This book is designed to help a serious investor make money. I believe it is the only book a serious investor needs to achieve his or her financial goals in the stock market. I have followed the rules laid out in the following chapters with much success, multiplying my investment capital many times over in the past ten years. There is little danger of this approach failing to operate in the future; neither do I fear that disclosing my "system" will make it useless because everyone will be able to use it. These dangers are minimal because investors in general are never going to be willing to submit themselves to the discipline required by my methods, nor will they be willing to exercise the patience which is equally important. This book is written for those investors with the requisite patience and discipline, who need only to be shown how to apply those traits to make money.

I learned the lessons in this book over a period of 28 years of bull and bear markets. The book should help others succeed without spending as many years as I did in the school of experience. Before being nominated for sainthood, I should point out that I expect to make money from this book. So will you.

ACKNOWLEDGMENTS

This book was "stric'ly my own idea." The idea could not have become a book without some important help and encouragement, however. My father, Theodore J. Seiver, read the first and second drafts of the entire manuscript and made many useful comments. My colleague, Dennis H.

Sullivan, made copious and valuable comments on all chapters of this book and also provided constant encouragement. Another colleague, Donald J. Cymrot, read the first draft and also made some valuable suggestions which I incorporated into the text. Jeff Krames, of Prentice-Hall, created the cover design and gave me a new (and better) title to go with it. Barbara Seiver, who has a controlling interest in the author, displayed the requisite patience and discipline during the inevitable "crunches." My children, Elizabeth and Robert, were rightly oblivious the whole time. Heartfelt thanks to all.

1

INTRODUCTION

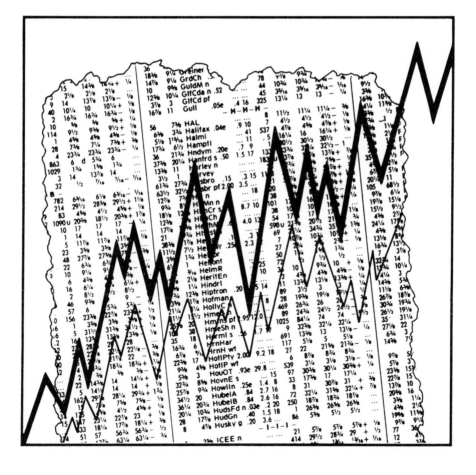

A. THE SECRET: PATIENCE AND DISCIPLINE (PAD)

The secret of *Outperforming Wall Street* is simple: Patience and Discipline. These two traits are so important I have elevated them to a "system": the P(atience) A(nd) D(iscipline) System or the PAD System for short. If you have patience and can discipline yourself to follow rules, you have the two most important qualities of a successful investor. These traits cannot be learned. Everything else you need can be learned from this book.

B. OUTLINE OF THE BOOK

The first foundation stone of stock market success is individual stock selection. Picking stocks that outperform the market is half the battle, albeit a difficult one. In Chapter 2, I set out the rules I use to pick stocks that will outperform the market over the long run, that is, the next three to five years. I explain in Chapter 7 why I believe this is the only time horizon that will permit the ordinary investor to consistently beat the market. The rules are objective criteria that a company's stock must satisfy before it can be included in a PAD investor's portfolio. As I explain later, it is only necessary to sift through a small number of growth stocks, so the selection process is not especially time consuming.

The stocks that end up in your portfolio will normally stay there for a number of years. This is why patience is so important. Many investors buy good growth stocks and then do not wait for them to grow.

An Appendix to Chapter 2 contains a list and discussion of PAD stocks that have met all or most of the selection criteria in the past. Some of these stocks, including my favorites, will probably not meet all the criteria when this book is read, however. The best uses of the list and discussion are as "hands on" examples of the selection process.

Chapter 3 explains the best way to buy a stock that has passed all the tests of Chapter 2. I recommend using discount brokers, and an Appendix to the chapter contains information and advice on choosing a discount broker.

I also present rules for selling stocks, both those that have done well and those that have not. Neither selling decision is easy, and most investment advice is geared toward finding winners, rather than dealing with the inevitable losers. Chapters 2 and 3 also contain some examples, called "Case Histories," of the application of the rules I set out, taken from my own investment experience.

In Chapter 4 I describe my techniques of market timing, the other foundation stone of successful PAD investing. I draw on fundamental, technical, and psychological indicators to try to avoid either buying during periods of market overvaluation or selling during periods of market undervaluation. This is a very difficult task, mainly because it is so hard to avoid being swept along with the herd of ordinary investors, whose panic selling creates buying opportunities and whose greed drives stocks to unsustainable levels. The herd instinct is not confined to the lower echelons of the investing world, either. The "Nifty Fifty" of the early 1970s were the overpriced darlings of institutional investors until the bubble burst in 1974.

The health of the economy has a crucial impact on the health of the stock market. To understand all the interrelationships among money, credit, interest rates, deficits, inflation, and economic growth requires more than the 18 pages I devote to it in Chapter 5. But my brief discussion should be sufficient to direct you toward real knowledge of how the economy works, which should put you near the top of Wall Street's knowledge pyramid. In addition, your understanding of economic trends should improve your timing decisions in the stock market.

The long-run trend of economic growth in the United States is just as important to the PAD investor. In Chapter 6, I present my scenario for the U.S. economy for the rest of the century. It is basically a rosy view, although I do discuss many of the current and future dangers the economy must face. The bright future I see is in part a result of the electronic revolution we are experiencing in the 1980s, and the stocks that will be in the PAD investor's portfolio are in the forefront of this revolution. My forecast for the future is the basis for concentrating investments in high-technology stocks.

Although economists have made significant contributions to our understanding of the economy, many of them believe in "efficient markets" theory. A key inference of the main variant of this theory is that it is virtually impossible for any investor to beat the market consistently. Obviously I disagree. Yet it would be a mistake to dismiss the theory out of hand, as many on Wall Street have done, since another variant of the theory is probably true. I explain both variants in a nontechnical fashion in Chapter 7, and point out the various flaws in the theory, using recent research by economists themselves as my chief weapon of attack. This recent research serves double duty, since it also provides a theoretical justification for the PAD system itself.

Some investors, especially conservative ones, may be unwilling to limit their portfolio to PAD stocks, even though they want to use the PAD system. In Chapter 8, I present a modified set of rules that preserves the spirit of the PAD system, while applying it to a much wider universe of stocks. On the other hand, some growth stock investors may consider PAD stocks to be too stodgy. I present another variation on the PAD theme for them in the second part of Chapter 8. The PAD rules, with modifications, can be used to help a more aggressive investor build a PAD portfolio out of more volatile stocks reviewed by the Value Line OTC Special Situations Service.

In Chapter 9, I describe the essential elements of options and financial futures trading. I recommend conservative strategies that enable a PAD investor to "insure" his or her portfolio from a market decline without being forced to sell stock from the portfolio. This strategy is recommended only for the experienced PAD investor with a substantial portfolio.

In Chapter 10, I have collected a useful and diverse set of odds and ends—little tidbits of knowledge and advice which are helpful, but don't really fit in to the basic story: tax strategy, IRAs, recordkeeping, etc. Chapter 11 contains some concluding comments.

C. CAUTIONS

A few words of caution before we begin. You cannot buy stock without money. This is not a "nothing down" book. If you do not have at least $5000 to invest, you cannot take full advantage of the PAD system. And the money has to be invested for a number of years. That means you can't invest the rent money! I also do not recommend that any investor put all of his or her assets in the stock market, no matter how much you love this book. Your own home is a good investment, and a rainy day fund kept in a money market mutual fund is an excellent investment. While this advice has certainly become a cliché, it is still true. I also do not recommend that you devote all of your free time to the stock market. Having other hobbies will help you maintain the detachment necessary for patience and discipline. Applying the basic PAD System of Chapters 2–4 should only take about 3 hours per week. Additional time can be spent monitoring the economy (Chapters 5 and 6), insuring a large portfolio (Chapter 9), and minimizing taxes (Chapter 10).*

D. A LITTLE TEST

A final word of caution: some readers will have great difficulty becoming PAD investors. To test your potential, answer the following four questions honestly:

1. Does your spending regularly exceed your income?
2. Do you agonize over small decisions?
3. Do you think a person's income and assets are the best measures of what a person is "worth" in life?
4. Is the stock market your only hobby?

If you answered with four resounding "no"s, this book should suit you perfectly. If you answered "yes" four times, you may have to change your way of life before you can profit from this book. If you answered both "yes" and "no," read on and decide for yourself.

---

*Information on updates and enhancements to the PAD System can be found in Chapter 10, Section F.6.

2

INDIVIDUAL
STOCK SELECTION

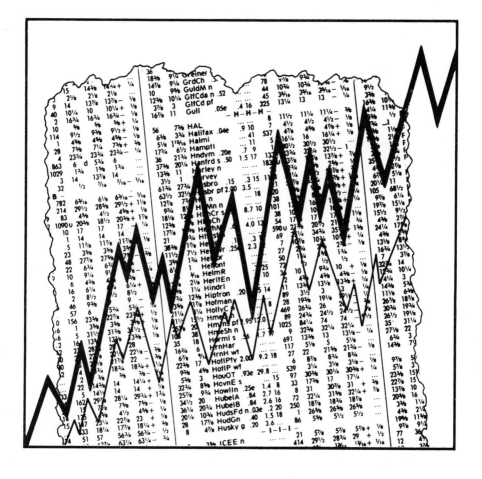

The two great investment battles you must fight are (1) finding stocks that tend to do better than the market over the long run, and (2) buying when stocks are cheap and selling when they are dear. It is not necessary to win both battles all the time, but regular losses on one battle front can cost you the war for investment success. Almost all stocks fall sharply in a bear market, whether they are good, bad, or ugly. Chapters 2 and 3 are designed to help you buy and sell individual stocks that will outperform the market. Chapter 4 is designed to improve your market timing, that is, to help you identify periods of undervaluation and overvaluation in the market as a whole. Selection and timing are obviously not exact sciences, but with patience and the discipline of the rules I will set out, you can improve your chances of success. If you feel you are already accomplished in one category or the other, you should just skim the relevant chapter(s) to see whether you might have overlooked an idea or two that might improve your performance further. If you are regularly winning both these battles, you should be writing a book on the stock market yourself!

A. THE FUNDAMENTAL APPROACH

What Wall Streeters mean by "fundamentals" is the study and evaluation of stocks in terms of their current and future earnings and dividends, and their balance sheets. Studying stocks in this manner is beyond the means of the nonprofessional investor. The time requirements and the skills necessary to decode published reports of income statements and assets and liabilities are substantial. For these reasons, masses of analyses are done by professionals and sold to the public, both by brokerage firms, which publish research reports, and by firms that produce only research.

While many brokerage firms produce valuable research and do a good job for their clients, their commission structure is much higher than discount brokers, who provide the customer with just two services: the execution of buy and sell orders, and market quotations. The full-service brokerage firm and its brokers make money when clients trade, and this creates a conflict of interest when they are also providing advice. Since this book is designed to help you make your own decisions, it follows naturally that you should deal with a discount broker and save commissions, and use research services to help you select stocks. Discount brokers and the PAD approach to buying and selling are discussed in Chapter 3 and its Appendix.

Where do we get access to the research we need to make informed stock decisions? In my 28 years of investment experience, I have never found a better source of data and interpretation than the *Value Line Investment Survey* (VLIS).*

If you are not familiar with VLIS, I suggest you look at a recent weekly issue before reading any further, because Value Line forms the basis of the PAD fundamental approach to stock selection.

My high regard for Value Line is shared by many others. Professor Fischer Black of M.I.T., who has espoused the view that no one can either predict or "beat" the markets, has stated that research departments should fire all their stock analysts except one, and give that one a subscription to Value Line. (Black left M.I.T. for a job on Wall Street with Goldman, Sachs. I do not know if he subscribes to Value Line.) The basis for this high praise from a skeptical academic is Value Line's consistent ability

---

*I have never had, nor do I ever intend to have, any relationship, financial or otherwise, with Value Line, Inc., or any of its employees. I do keep IRA and TSA money in Value Line mutual funds.

to predict which groups of stocks will perform better than others. In addition to forecasting the relative short-term performances of all of the companies it covers, Value Line also provides and interprets masses of individual company and economy-wide data which are beyond any individual's capability to analyze.

The weekly VLIS comes in three parts. First, there is the "Value Line View," which reviews general trends in the market, picks a "Stock of the Week," and usually covers some special topic in brief. The second and most important part is the full-page reviews of the 1,700 stocks covered by VLIS, each reviewed four times a year. Since new developments can affect Value Line's opinion about a company at any time, there are supplementary reports on a number of different stocks every week, usually those involved in mergers or buyouts, or those reporting unexpectedly good or bad profits. The third part, called the "Summary Index," includes current rankings for every stock every week.

While Value Line has demonstrated that it is capable of predicting the relative price performances of groups of stocks, I do not believe the firm has shown much ability to forecast general trends in the market. (The company admits as much, but also asserts that no one else can, either.) Thus, the real value of Value Line to the PAD investor is the sifting and analyzing of all the fundamental information about a stock, resulting in a forecast for the given company over the following year and a projection for the three-to-five-year time horizon, which is the time horizon for the PAD investor. It is not necessary, however, to review all 1,700 stocks monitored by Value Line. The PAD investor can concentrate on just a few high-growth industries I discuss below.

As I point out in Chapter 6, the next fifteen years will be a period of accelerated change in the American economy. In general, we tend to underestimate the amount of change that will take place. The most important changes will be technological, and those companies that supply the products that fuel those changes will see their sales and earnings rise dramatically if they are not mismanaged. It should be no surprise that computers, electronics, and precision instruments are three industries that I think will continue to grow incredibly fast for the foreseeable future, and investors in these industries will be suitably rewarded. Value Line can help you select and monitor the stocks in these industries so that you participate fully in future growth.

In 1983, Wall Street was in full agreement with this rosy scenario, and bid up all high-technology stocks to unsustainable levels. By the spring of 1985, a true slowdown in the rate of growth of these industries, combined with falling profits and even losses for some companies, changed the sentiment on Wall Street completely, and high-technology stocks were driven down to unreasonably low levels. This created a buying opportunity for those who could resist the violent mood swings and herd instinct of Wall Street. The 1983–86 high-technology bear market also serves as a cautionary note to PAD investors that there will be violent ups and downs and trying times in the future. You must keep your head while others are losing theirs.

B. STOCK SELECTION RULES

How can you tell which stocks in the computer, electronics, and precision instruments industries will be tomorrow's winners? The most important considerations are (1) future growth of earnings, and (2) the valuation of those earnings, i.e., the so-called price–earnings (*p/e*) ratio. Let me illustrate with a simple example. Suppose stock X is selling for $10 a share. Suppose also that Value Line is estimating that the company will earn $1.00 per share this year. Then the stock's current *p/e* ratio, which is just price divided by per share earnings, is 10. Now if this company were to double its earnings next year, to $2.00 a share, and were to still sell for 10 times earnings (*p/e*=10), the company's stock would then sell for $20 a share. If, on the other hand, the company earned only $1.00 a share next year, but its *p/e* ratio rose to 20, the stock would also sell for 20. In either case, we have the happy result that the stock doubled. But in the second case, this is only because the market is valuing the earnings at a much higher level. Price–earnings ratios for stocks in general tend to rise during bull markets and fall during bear markets. Thus, the stock of a company earning $1.00 a share year after year will tend to rise and fall with the market, but after several years it will still probably sell for about the same price. On the other hand, a company with growing earnings, although it will also be buffeted by bull and bear markets, should eventually sell for a higher price, based on its higher earnings.

Now it is of course true that the market valuation should reflect what the company's prospects are for the future, but this is not always the case. Often during bull markets, the price–earnings ratio for many stocks expands beyond reason, such that investors pay $50 or $100 or more for $1.00 of earnings today. Future earnings would have to rise at an almost impossible rate for the current price to make sense. Turning the *p/e* on its head, that is, inverting it to make it become an earnings–price ratio, makes this clearer: $1.00 of earnings divided by a price of $20 is .05, or 5 percent. We can think of this as the earnings yield on our investment of $20. When the same stock is selling for $100, the earnings yield is a minuscule 1 percent, incredibly small, and acceptable to investors for only short periods of time. If the company does achieve earnings of, say, $2.00 a share two years later, but the *p/e* drops to 20, or an earnings yield of 5 percent, the stock will fall from $100 to $40!

During bear markets, *p/e* ratios often shrink to very low levels, which are just as unrealistic and temporary. When the mood of extreme pessimism ends, stocks rise as *p/e*'s expand, and those companies with rising earnings will thus get a double boost to their prices.

Of course, it is impossible for the individual investor to forecast the earnings or the price–earnings ratios of individual stocks. But Value Line does do this for about four years into the future, which is beyond the time horizon of most investors. Combining future earnings and a price–earnings ratio, Value Line estimates a future average price and a range around it, reflecting the changing moods of Wall Street. This range, called the "3–5 year appreciation potential," is one of the most important numbers in the Value Line full-page report on an individual stock. (See Figure 2.1, line A.) While this potential is clearly an educated guess, it provides an objective technique for selecting those stocks which should do well during the next several years.

RULE 1.   APPRECIATION POTENTIAL MUST BE AT LEAST 100 PERCENT TO THE LOW END OF THE RANGE.

A first rule for selecting stocks that will grow substantially is to find stocks that have at least a 100 percent appreciation potential to the low end of the range. (Digital's low-end potential is 120% in Figure 2.1). While it is all right to hold on to stocks that you already own with appreciation potentials below this benchmark, do not commit new funds to stocks that cannot meet this criterion.

RULE 2.   ESTIMATED FUTURE EARNINGS MUST BE AT LEAST 100 PERCENT HIGHER THAN EARNINGS OF THE MOST RECENTLY COMPLETED YEAR (OR THE ESTIMATE FOR THE YEAR IN PROGRESS).

Satisfying Rule 1 is only the first hurdle the prospective company must clear before you vote "yes" with your dollars. Some stocks with high

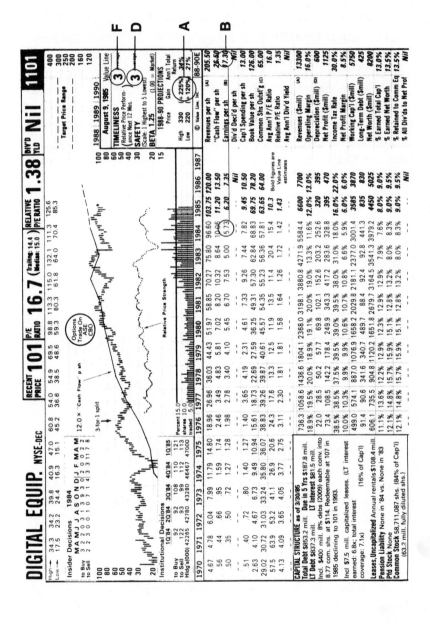

Figure 2.1 (Copyright 1985, Value Line, Inc. Reprinted with permission.)

CURRENT POSITION ($ Mill.)	1983	1984	3/30/85
Cash Assets	556.2	476.2	898.9
Receivables	1125.1	1527.2	1484.7
Inventory(FIFO)	1353.8	1852.2	2017.8
Other	166.3	226.3	253.3
Current Assets	3201.4	4081.9	4654.7
Accts Payable	213.7	278.1	175.5
Debt Due	16.3	14.6	15.9
Other	594.4	787.8	869.5
Current Liab.	824.4	1080.5	1060.9

ANNUAL RATES of change (per sh)	Past 10 Yrs	Past 5 Yrs	Est '82-'84 to '88-'90
Revenues	25.0%	17.5%	17.0%
"Cash Flow"	24.5%	15.5%	18.5%
Earnings	22.0%	12.0%	19.0%
Dividends	—	—	Nil
Book Value	24.5%	22.5%	12.0%

QUARTERLY REVENUES ($ mill.) Fiscal Year Ends	Sept. 30	Dec. 31	Mar. 31	June 30	Full Fiscal Year
1982	839.4	965.8	999.3	1076.3	3880.8
1983	927.5	1015.7	1094.3	1234.4	4271.9
1984	1074.4	1423.8	1430.8	1655.4	5584.4
1985	1515.3	1628.1	1691.1	1765.5	6600
1986	1600	1800	2000	2300	7700

EARNINGS PER SHARE (A) (B) Fiscal Year Ends	Sept. 30	Dec. 31	Mar. 31	June 30	Full Fiscal Year
1982	1.60	1.79	1.94	2.20	7.53
1983	1.02	1.08	1.40	1.50	5.00
1984	.28	1.41	1.76	2.28	5.73
1985	1.38	1.81	1.52	1.49	6.20
1986	1.40	1.65	1.90	2.40	7.35

QUARTERLY DIVIDENDS PAID (C) Cal-endar	Mar. 31	June 30	Sept. 30	Dec. 31	Full Year
1981					
1982		NO CASH DIVIDENDS			
1983		BEING PAID			
1984					
1985					

(A) Fiscal year ends about June 30th of calendar year. (B) Fully diluted. Excludes nonrecurring gain: '85, $1.07. Next earnings report due mid-Aug. Estimated current cost egs./sh.: '84, $7.65/sh. (C) In millions, adjusted for stock splits. (D) Depreciation on accelerated basis.

BUSINESS: Digital Equipment Corporation is the leading manufacturer of small digital computers (minicomputers). Ranks about 2nd in information processing industry revenues. Applications include research, education, industrial control, timesharing, commercial data processing, word processing, health care, instrumentation, engineering, simulation. Service income comprises 31% of revenue; foreign business, 35%. U.S. gov't 5%. R&D equals 11.3% of rev.; payroll costs, est'd 40%. '84 dep. rate: 10.8%. Est'd plant age: 3 yrs. Has 89,200 employees, 43,350 shareholders. Insiders control 6% of stock. President: K.H. Olsen. Inc.: Massachusetts. Address: 146 Main St., Maynard, MA 01754.

We've lowered our sights for DEC again. Sales of the new top-of-the-line Venus (VAX 8600) and the new low-end MicroVAX II have been strong, but not strong enough to overcome the weakness in the rest of the line. We expect revenues to be up from the March quarter, but continued high production and sales expenses, and increased interest expense, will keep pressure on earnings. Results won't be announced until after we've gone to press, but we've cut our share earnings estimate for the 1985 fiscal year (ended June 29th) to $6.20, from $6.50.

We expect a slow start for fiscal 1986. It looks as if capital spending, especially for computer equipment, in the United States will be restrained for the rest of calendar 1985, as customers digest their existing computer power and mull over the many new choices available. And in Europe, things could weaken. Although Digital hasn't reported any problems, others have, and there is no reason to believe DEC is immune. Moreover, we don't expect an early widening of margins. Management has announced plans to cut costs but, given its policy of using attrition, rather than layoffs, to reduce personnel, it will take time.

Things should speed up in the second half of fiscal 1986. Digital has invested heavily in research and development and in its sales team over the last several years. Venus and MicroVAX give DEC one of the broadest ranges of computer power in the industry; customers can move up the line without the expense of rewriting software. At the high end, computers can be linked together in a "VAXCluster," which gives the user mainframe power at a minicomputer price. And the low-end Microvax II will open new markets in the computer-aided engineering field. The new markets and upward migration from its current user base of 40,000 VAX systems will drive revenues to record highs. If management's focus on cost control is successful, share earnings will rise even faster.

But this may not be the time to buy Digital's shares. However, we think DEC's investment in new products and in its sales force will support substantial capital appreciation for these shares over the longer haul. And if cost cutting takes hold faster than we expect, accelerated share price appreciation would follow.

G.A.N./L.K.

Company's Financial Strength	A++
Stock's Price Stability	40
Price Growth Persistence	60
Earnings Predictability	65

Figure 2.1 (*continued*)

appreciation potential are not forecast to have much higher earnings, but just a much higher price–earnings ratio. These stocks are immediately suspect, because their future appreciation is dependent mainly upon the market placing a higher valuation on the current level of earnings, rather than on a significant rise in earnings. Value Line will often project a higher *p/e* ratio than the current one if the historical data show that the *p/e* ratio tended to be higher in the past than at the current time. But betting on

---

CASE HISTORY: FAIRCHILD CAMERA AND INSTRUMENT
(Figure 2.2)

I first purchased FCI in 1974. This company was one of the original high-technology companies of Silicon Valley. Many of its employees went on to start successful electronics companies, but FCI's earnings foundered in spite of its technological excellence. I purchased additional shares in 1977, when the stock was depressed partly by negative reports in the *Wall Street Journal*. Patience and discipline paid off when FCI was purchased by Schlumberger in 1980. See Chapter 3's merger and buyout section for a discussion of strategies for these situations.

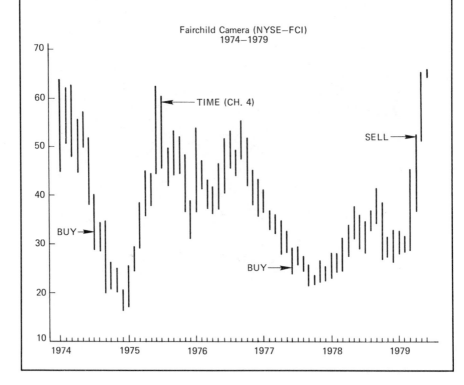

Fairchild Camera (NYSE–FCI)
1974–1979

a change in the *p/e* ratio means betting on a change in mood on Wall Street, and that, in my opinion, is too much of a gamble.

Future earnings are marked in Figure 2.1 at line B. Estimated future earnings should be at least twice the level for the most recently completed year to ensure that a large portion of the appreciation potential represents growth rather than revaluation of earnings.

This level test cannot be applied if the most recently completed year resulted in a loss or abnormally low earnings. In such a situation, the Value Line estimate for the year in progress, which appears in a column adjacent to the data for the previous year, should be used as a base for performing the 100 percent test. If both years are abnormally depressed, the stock is disqualified from consideration for purchase.

The ability of management is a key ingredient in reaching the doubling goal. Many high-technology companies produce exciting new products with great prospects and no earnings growth to show for it, reflecting the inability of management to bring the sales dollars down to the bottom line. How can you detect management problems? There are two hints from the history of earnings section of the Value Line stock report: if there have been either repeated years of losses in the past, or frequent wild fluctuations in earnings, I would be cautious, although I have not formalized this notion into a rule.

RULE 3:   A FINANCIAL STRENGTH RATING BELOW "B" OR A SAFETY RATING OF "5" (LOWEST) DISQUALIFIES THE COMPANY.

We also want to sift out firms that could not survive a temporary setback in their fortunes. Toward that end, VLIS reports a financial strength rating and a safety rating (Figure 2.1, lines C and D). These ratings reflect detailed analyses of cash flow, composition of debt and its size relative to equity (leverage), and other balance sheet items which I find are best left to Value Line to interpret. If either of these ratings are at the low end for all VLIS stocks, the company is probably too risky.

RULE 4:   R&D PERCENTAGE MUST BE AT LEAST 7.5 PERCENT.

If a particular stock is still in the running, the next important statistic is the percentage of sales going to research and development (R&D). This crucial statistic is buried in the center of the full-page report (Figure 2.1, line E). For most growing high-technology companies, the products that will make up the bulk of sales five years from now are not on the market yet. The best indication of the probability of successful new products and innovations is the percent set aside today to create tomorrow's products. My rule here is that R&D must be at least 7.5% of sales, or the company is disqualified, on the grounds that its competitive chances are weakened and its growth prospects are reduced significantly.

Some companies have significant amounts of customer-sponsored research and development. This is not nearly as valuable a sign of technological commitment, since the company is not putting aside its own funds for the future. Thus, only company-funded R&D should be counted toward satisfaction of this rule. (Value Line reports the two R&D figures separately.)

Even in hard times, companies should maintain the 7.5 percentage if they have confidence in the future. Thus, there should be no exception to this rule. If, however, a company whose stock you have purchased reduces its R&D spending below this level, it should not be sold immediately, but should be considered a candidate for sale when market conditions match those discussed in Chapter 4.

RULE 5:   SHORT-TERM PERFORMANCE RANKING MUST BE HIGHER THAN "5" (LOWEST).

Stocks that meet all of these stringent requirements will be in your portfolio at some time. But clearing these hurdles is still not sufficient to merit an immediate *buy*. First, we must consider market timing, which is discussed in Chapter 4. Buying PAD stocks when the market is about to begin a major decline is not going to be very profitable. They will decline with the rest of the market, and perhaps even faster. So you must review timing considerations. Just as important, the current prospects of these PAD companies may be especially clouded, leading you to avoid them until a more appropriate time. How can one tell? Value Line also computes a short-term (one-year) performance rating for all stocks, from 1 (highest) to 5 (lowest). Stocks that are rated 5 for year-ahead performance should probably be avoided. There is usually a good reason for this low ranking: a severe earnings decline, or uncertain prospects over the next few months (new competition, major litigation, or internal restructuring, for example).

As mentioned above, Value Line's reputation has been built partly on its ability to discriminate among stock groups over a period of a year or less. Since it has repeatedly demonstrated that stocks with low rankings tend to do worse on average than stocks with high rankings, it is wise to use this information in timing your PAD purchases, even though you plan to hold stocks much more than one year.

Stocks ranked 1, 2, or 3 can be bought without hesitation if market timing suggests that the market is not headed down. Stocks ranked 4 are more problematic. I would go ahead if everything else about the company is satisfactory. For those stocks ranked 4 or 5 for year-ahead performance, but with future possibilities that are good, it is possible to use a form of technical analysis, discussed in Section E, to buy before the performance ranking improves, and before the stock moves up in price substantially.

It has been true in recent years that stocks ranked 4 and 5 have done very well in the first weeks of a new year. This is no doubt the result of tax-loss selling at the end of the year, driving these stocks down to unreasonable levels. This is obviously a good time to buy them. Tax-loss selling and strategy are discussed further in Chapter 10.

It is a good idea to scan Value Line every week, even though your current and future portfolio stocks are reviewed only once every three months. Value Line's opinions, particularly for short-term performance, often change more frequently than that. Supplementary reports, which may involve substantial changes in opinion, can be issued at any time. But as a PAD investor, you will not be influenced by short-term changes in either your stocks, the market, or VL opinions. Additional uses of the VLIS are discussed in Chapters 3 and 4.

C. DIVIDENDS

I have not discussed dividends for good reason. The stocks the PAD investor will buy often pay no dividends. None will ever be paying out a large portion of dividends to stockholders because the earnings are being reinvested in the business. I consider a large share of earnings paid out in dividends to be a sure sign of maturity and poor growth prospects. Stock dividend yields do not compete with bond yields or any other yields, nor do future dividends really determine the price of a stock, contrary to what some investment analysts have written. One good example should suffice. Digital Equipment, the second largest computer manufacturer, has never paid a dividend, and probably never will, based on corporate policy. Yet it has often sold for over $100 a share! What is holding it up? Earnings growth in the future and the capital gains that it is likely to bring. Earnings growth will drive up the price even with a constant *p/e* ratio. Imagine a corporate raider attempting to buy up the company. He might pay much more than $100 to get the future income stream the company will generate in the form of after-tax profits. If this argument is not sufficient to convince you, consider the tax consequences of dividends, which are taxed as ordinary income (after a paltry exclusion), versus long-term capital gains, taxed for many years at half or at less than half the tax rate on ordinary income. In fact, it is very difficult to explain why firms do pay dividends, given the tax consequences. Those companies which are almost solely income vehicles, such as the public utilities, are exceptions to the rule of dividend irrelevance. Their shares are very similar to bonds, and are tied closely to interest rates. But these kinds of companies will never be in the PAD investor's portfolio.

D. OTHER FUNDAMENTAL APPROACHES

I have purposely avoided any detailed discussion of balance sheets and net worth. Value Line will alert you if there are serious problems in this area (Rule 3). A good growth stock will rarely sell below book value per share, but that does not matter. The PAD system will not uncover "turnaround" or especially undervalued stocks.

I am not suggesting that other fundamental methods of stock analysis and selection are worthless. They clearly are not. There are many groups of stocks that are undervalued at one time or another, depending on the mood on Wall Street. In general, out-of-favor stocks usually come back into favor, rewarding investors who go against the trend. Even companies in Chapter 11 bankruptcy may be quite profitable as investments, but they will not qualify as PAD stocks.

E. TECHNICAL ANALYSIS

Technicians on Wall Street are not at all interested in any of the foregoing discussion. It is their belief that movements of a stock's price, volume of trading, relative strength of a stock compared to the market in general and other even more obscure measures, are the best indications of the future trend of a stock's price. A true technician does not even need to know the name of the company or its business. I was once, at a very impressionable age, a technician of the chartist persuasion. Now older and wiser, I have very little faith in the ability of technical analysis alone to help investors. The only situation in which I think it can be useful is in timing purchases of those stocks, selected with the rules listed above, that are poorly ranked for year-ahead performance.

It should be no surprise that insiders will detect a turnaround in a company's fortunes before the general public or even Value Line is aware of it. To take advantage of their knowledge, those who know often buy the stock, and the price pattern of the stock may reveal this buying. Stripping away all the mysticism surrounding charting, we can note that stocks usually fall, then stop falling, then start going up, then stop going up, and then start falling. Most of technical analysis is designed to determine when these major changes in direction will take place. A PAD stock that is suffering earnings reversals will probably stop falling and start going up before there is an announcement of higher earnings. A chart of the price can reveal this pattern, and justify a *buy* even though VL may still rate the company a 4 for near-term performance.

The two most common kinds of charts are point-and-figure and bar charts. Many others exist, each with its loyal following. There are many books available in libraries which can explain how to construct these charts, and I will restrict the discussion here to one example based on my own experience.

The key features to look for in a bar chart or a point-and-figure chart are the appearance of sideways movement after a decline. Then, when the stock starts to move up, it is time to *buy*.

For those readers who find this approach irresistibly appealing, as I did in my callow youth, total immersion in technical analysis, followed by complete disillusionment, is probably the best medicine. One can purchase a compendium of technical analysis from Chartcraft, Inc. which should satisfy the appetite of even the truest gnome or elf of Wall Street. However, with the one exception I have discussed, I cannot recommend technical analysis for a PAD investor. Many stocks have short, violent downswings during the course of a long-term rise to much higher levels. Thus, even if the chart turns bearish, relative strength weakens, and the stock falls below its two-hundred-day moving average, you should continue to hold. There are too many false signals given by every technical method I know for them to be of any general use. Note that the point-and-figure chart of Genrad gave several sell signals during its rapid ascent. Technical indicators of *general* market trends are much more useful. They are discussed in Chapter 4.

CASE HISTORY: GENRAD
(Figure 2.3)

Genrad, Inc. is one of the stocks listed at the end of this chapter which has
in the past met all of the preceding fundamental criteria. I purchased it
first, however, in April, 1982, when it was not favorably ranked by VLIS
for short-term performance, but the stock chart suggested that the earnings turnaround was coming. The arrows on the point-and-figure chart and
the bar chart mark my purchase decision. I sold half of my holding eleven
months later, after the stock had almost tripled. The stock continued to rise
for a while, but has since retraced all of its rise. (Bar-chart prices adjusted
for 3-for-2 split.)

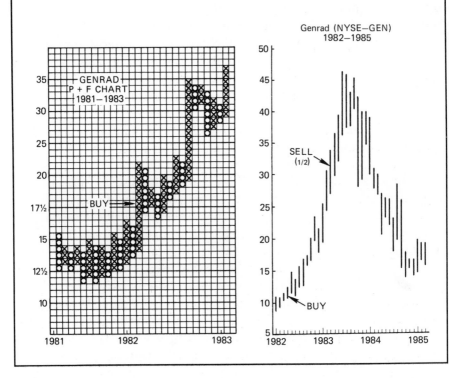

F. PORTFOLIO MANAGEMENT

1. Diversification

RULE 6: DIVERSIFY!

Any stock which qualifies as a PAD stock is a somewhat risky investment in two senses: (1) the stock is likely to fluctuate more than the general market, so that if the market goes down, it will fall by a greater percentage; and (2) the prospects for the stock's future are more uncertain than for other stocks in mature industries subject to much slower rates of technological change. For these reasons, you should not put all your eggs in one basket; that is, you need to hold a portfolio of several stocks almost all the time, unless, in anticipation of a bear market, you have been switching to cash, as explained in the next chapter.

The benefits of diversification can be understood without recourse to serious mathematics. Consider the following example. You have selected five stocks, using the rules listed above. Let's call them stocks A, B, C, D, and E. Suppose that in fact four of these stocks will double in the next two years, and one will drop to zero. (You must be prepared to take some losses when you make a mistake.) If you bought just one of the five, your portfolio would have a 4 out of 5 chance to increase by 100% and a 1 in 5 chance to fall by 100%. So if you played this game over and over, you would average gains of 60%. Not bad, but you only get to play the game once, and either you gain 100% or lose it all. If, instead, you buy all five of the stocks, you will certainly have one that falls to zero, but you will have four that double and you will make 60% every time! You have diversified away the risk of a disaster in this simple example, although you have given up the chance to make a 100% killing.*

This example is oversimplified, but it still shows the benefits of diversification. I believe you can diversify with as little as $5,000 spread over five stocks, although $20,000 spread over five to 10 stocks would probably be better.

If you have a $50,000 portfolio, or your $5,000 portfolio grows to $50,000, you can achieve greater diversification by holding more stocks.

---

*We have assumed in this example that what happens to Stock A has no effect on Stocks B through E, which will clearly not hold for the PAD investor, but we have also assumed that the portfolio cannot be managed to weed out losers. The example is strictly meant for exposition.

I have set out some rough guidelines in Table 2.1 which relate size of portfolio to number of stocks held when fully invested. If you keep within the guidelines for your portfolio size, in terms of both number of stocks held and dollar amount per stock, you can be diversified without being spread too thinly. I would initially invest roughly equal amounts in each stock; for example, a ten-stock portfolio bought with $50,000 should have about $5,000 invested in each stock. This rough equality will no doubt disappear as your stocks follow divergent paths, but when you add new stocks, you can again invest a proportional amount. For example, if your $50,000 portfolio has grown to $75,000, and you have $15,000 in cash ready to invest, you could buy two new stocks, putting about $7,500 in each, or three new stocks, putting about $5,000 in each. You would buy at least enough new stocks to maintain a ten-stock portfolio, the minimum for this size portfolio, and you would not let your total number of stocks rise above 15, which, if it did, would put your dollars per stock ($75,000/15) below the minimum of $5,000 for this portfolio size. The limits are broad enough to make it easy to stay within the recommended ranges for number of stocks and dollars per stock for your portfolio size. I have set a maximum of 20 stocks for any size portfolio, in the belief that this is large enough to reap all the benefits of diversification while still keeping investing as a hobby.

TABLE 2.1   Recommended Diversification

Portfolio Size ($)	Number of Stocks	$ Per Stock
$5,000–$10,000	5	$1,000–$2,000
$10,000–$50,000	5–10	$2,000–$5,000
$50,000–$200,000	10–20	$5,000–$10,000
over $200,000	20	over $10,000

2. The Buy List

The stocks you buy will come from your Buy List, which comprises those stocks which satisfy all of the rules of this chapter. Those which nearly satisfy all of the rules should be watched carefully, because minor market movements could make them full-fledged buys. With the one exception of "switches" (see Chapter 3), you will buy your Buy List stocks only when the market timing indicators of Chapter 4 are favorable. If the size of the list corresponds to the range of stocks which matches your portfolio size (see Table 2.1), you can buy all of your Buy List stocks following the rules of Chapter 3.

It may happen, however, that there are only two or three stocks on your Buy List when your market timing indicators signal *"buy,"* and you have a high level of cash reserves. Committing all of your cash reserves to these few stocks could then drive your dollars per stock level above the maximum in the table. While this is an unlikely problem, the solution is straightforward: buy only those on the Buy List, in amounts consistent with Table 2.1, and hold cash reserves until more stocks appear on the Buy List.

It is also possible that the purchase of all Buy List stocks would make your portfolio exceed the maximum recommended number of stocks. In this situation, you must be more selective. Although I present no rules for this pleasant dilemma, I have solved it by raising my standards until the number of stocks on the Buy List has dropped to the point where I can buy all of them. Rule 5 is my first choice for upgrading, making either a "3" or a "2" (truly picky) a requirement for short-term performance. This upgrade will normally be sufficient, but if not, I would upgrade Rule 1 until the list has shrunk sufficiently.

3. Mutual Funds as an Alternative

A representative group of PAD stocks is included in the appendix to this chapter. While many of these stocks are, and will continue to be, in my PAD portfolio, circumstances change. The reader can use the discussion of each stock in the appendix to see how I have applied the rules of this chapter in the past, but purchase decisions must be based on current Value Line reports. If this still seems too daunting a task, or if the risks of individual stock selection seem too great, consider "no-load" mutual funds as an alternative. There are a number of them which invest in growth or even technology stocks exclusively, and the charges made for managing your money are quite small. Investing in a mutual fund family which also has a cash fund would enable you to use the timing techniques of the next chapter, switching to cash to try to avoid the worst parts of the inevitable bear markets of the future. In spite of what salesmen will tell you, there is no evidence that mutual funds which charge front-end loads of up to 9 percent, called "load" funds, perform any better than no-loads.

The load charge is paid to the salesman for selling you the shares of the fund. No-load funds can be easily identified in the newspaper.*

In fact, a blend of mutual fund and individual stocks may be ideal until you have demonstrated to yourself that you are a talented stock picker.

SUMMARY OF RULES FOR THIS CHAPTER

1. Appreciation potential must be at least 100 percent to the low end of the range.
2. Estimated future earnings must be at least 100 percent higher than earnings of the most recently completed year (or the estimate for the year in progress).
3. A financial strength rating below "B" or a safety rating of "5" (lowest) disqualifies the company.
4. R&D percentage must be at least 7.5 percent.
5. Short-term performance ranking must be higher than "5" (lowest).
6. Diversify!

Readings for the PAD Investor

Encyclopedia of Stock Market Techniques. Published by Chartcraft/Investors Intelligence, 2 East Avenue, Larchmont, NY 10538. Includes several supplements. Has it all, including a high price ($60.00).

Value Line Investment Survey. Published weekly by Value Line, Inc., 711 Third Avenue, New York, NY 10017. My bible, available at many public and university libraries, or by subscription for $495 a year (in 1987). A must.

FISCHER BLACK, "Yes, Virginia, There is Hope: Tests of Value Line Ranking System," *Financial Analysts Journal,* September–October, 1973. An academic test of the Value Line ranking system.

THOMAS E. COPELAND AND DAVID MAYERS, "The Value Line Enigma (1965–1978)," *Journal of Financial Economics* 10 (November, 1982), pp. 289–321. There is still hope!

---

*Some "no-load" funds charge hefty fees under "Section 12b–1." Investigate before you invest. Value Line also provides pure no-load mutual funds without any sales charge.

APPENDIX: PAD STOCKS

The ten stocks listed below have often qualified as PAD stocks. All of them have been in my portfolio in the past, and many will no doubt be in my portfolio in the future. But this list can in no way substitute for the application of the PAD rules to current Value Line reports. I have also owned shares of many of the companies on the second list (see below). A PAD investor should review *all* of the stocks in PAD industries regularly.

MY TEN FAVORITE PAD STOCKS

Advanced Micro Devices, Inc.

This semiconductor stock has been spending more on R&D than most, and it has paid off in the form of new products. AMD was hurt by the electronics downturn of 1984–86, but it should recover as fast as its competitors. While it has often had a 3–5 year appreciation potential above 100 percent, it also has had a below average safety rating and a minimum rating for financial strength. The price tends to fluctuate more than most, so it is not for the faint of heart.

Amdahl

Amdahl makes mainframe computers that are compatible with IBM. The company was founded by Gene Amdahl, formerly a top IBM designer. He left to found still another company, but Amdahl has survived and prospered. They must run very hard to stay up with "Big Blue," but I think they have done it better than IBM's other mainframe competitors. Spending 16 percent on R&D is the key.

Analog Devices

Analog is a leading producer of integrated circuits with a wide range of applications. While it was not hit too hard by the 1984–86 downturn and is somewhat "safer" than many electronics stocks, it also is rarely available cheaply enough to pass the Rule 1 requirement.

Cray Research

Seymour Cray left Control data to found Cray Research. I found Cray some years ago, and now all of Wall Street has jumped on the bandwagon. As long as Cray is richly priced compared to its 3–5 year potential, it will not qualify for purchase. The discipline of Rule 1 forces the PAD investor to wait for the next Cray.

Digital Equipment

A full-page Value Line report on this company appears on pages 14 and 15. Note what happened to the price in October 1983 before you buy. When the institutional investors lose faith, watch out!

Hewlett-Packard

HP is a major force in electronics, computers, and precision instruments, a triple play. My only concern is that its prospects are heavily dependent on the success of its Spectrum line of computers.

Intel

Intel, one of the best known of the semiconductor manufacturers, is 20 percent owned by IBM. Their chips are used in IBM's microcomputers. Intel was hurt badly by the semiconductor slowdown, but if IBM continues to grow, Intel should grow too. IBM may reduce its stake in Intel, but I do not consider this possibility a cause for alarm.

Prime Computer

Prime was the star of the 1980 stock market. Since then, its earnings have improved while the stock price has languished. Continued earnings growth should translate into a higher stock price for this minicomputer manufacturer.

Tandem Computers

Tandem makes "fault-tolerant" computers that suffer almost no downtime. While sales tripled between 1981 and 1985, earnings were flat. If costs are controlled better in the future, the company's earnings and stock price could rise substantially. IBM is now a threat in this market, however.

Teradyne

Teradyne manufactures test equipment for the semiconductor industry and other industries. When semiconductors are good, Teradyne is very good, and when semiconductors are bad, Teradyne is horrid. Remember this PAD jingle before investing.

ADDITIONAL PAD STOCKS WITH HIGH R&D SPENDING (DO NOT OVERLOOK THESE COMPANIES!)

Electronics and Semiconductor

Applied Materials
Avantek
GCA Corp.
Genrad
Gould, Inc.
Kulicke and Soffa
Monolithic Memories
Motorola
National Semiconductor
Texas Instruments

Computers

Applied Magnetics
Centronics Data
Computervision
Data General
Gerber Scientific
Intergraph
Wang Labs

Precision Instruments

Coherent
Compugraphic
Eastman Kodak
Nicolet Instrument
Perkin-Elmer
Polaroid
Spectra-Physics
Tektronix

Note: Every year Value Line adds new stocks to its regular review schedule and removes others, so the list above is by no means exhaustive. In addition, I have omitted a few firms that spend more than 7.5 percent on R&D because there are other rules which they have almost never satisfied in the past.

3

BUYING AND
SELLING STOCKS

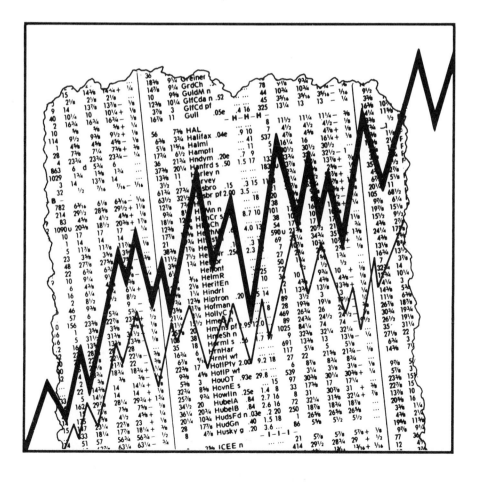

A. HOW TO BUY STOCK

RULE 1:   USE A DISCOUNT BROKER EXCLUSIVELY.

There is no point in paying a full-service broker for services such as research and advice when you are not going to use them. A discount broker will provide the basic service you need, and at a much lower commission cost. It is simple to open an account with a discount broker, and finding them is not hard either. Many advertise regularly in financial publications such as the *Wall Street Journal.* One element you sacrifice when you deal with a discount broker is the personal touch. You are dealing now with just a voice on the telephone, and usually a different one every time. But you can buy a hundred shares of stock for a fraction of the full-service charge. It's worth it. I would not deal with a firm which did not have its clients protected by SIPC, but major discount firms all have this protection. This, of course, does not mean that discount brokers cannot fail, any more than FDIC insurance means that banks will not fail. Bevill, Bressler, and Schulman failed in 1985, and their discount brokerage subsidiary was sold to another discount brokerage firm. While clients did not lose any money, and most were probably not inconvenienced at all, it is still a sobering reminder.

There is still another reason to use a discount broker. Srully Blotnick, in a study of 1,000 investors over the 1966–1976 period, discovered that many investors had complex psychological ties to their full-service brokers, and that the brokers had a fair amount of influence over the decisions of the investors. This can only work against a PAD investor, who must be as free as possible from the pressure to buy or sell or run with the herd. Blotnick's book is listed at the end of this chapter.

PAD investors unfamiliar with discount brokerage are urged to study the appendix to this chapter. It contains information and advice on choosing a discount broker.

RULE 2: BUY STOCKS ON YOUR BUY LIST AT FIXED INTERVALS.

When you have assembled your Buy List of PAD stocks, using the rules of Chapter 2, and the market timing indicators of Chapter 4 signal "*buy*," it is time to take your "shopping" list to the "store."

Since no one can call the turns in the market precisely, especially the short-term fluctuations which, if not completely inexplicable, are certainly unpredictable, a good strategy for purchasing stocks is to buy at fixed intervals. This is an important form of market discipline. If I am going to make a series of new investments, I restrict myself to one purchase a week or one purchase for every forty-point decline in the Dow-Jones Industrial Average from its level at the time of the previous purchase, whichever comes first. So if the market is not declining, you are restricted to one per week. During the final phase of a bear market, stocks often decline at a rapid rate, and thus your purchases will be accelerated, which will generally work in your favor. I also recheck each stock on my Buy List just before I buy it to make sure the stock is still a Buy.

RULE 3: DO NOT BUY ON MARGIN.

It is very tempting to consider enlarging your potential gains by purchasing stock on margin, which with a 50 percent requirement, increases your leverage by a factor of two, doubling your potential gains and losses. I recommend strongly against margin purchases for a patient investor with a 3–5 year time horizon. The biggest drawback to margin buying is the "margin call," a request by your broker to put up additional cash or securities to replenish your equity as your stocks decline. These calls force the investor's hand, and may result in forced liquidation of some or all of your portfolio if you cannot meet the margin call. PAD stocks may decline substantially before starting the long trek upward, and the investor who purchases them on margin just makes it more difficult to survive the hard times. These stocks are generally volatile enough to provide for sufficient excitement.

A simple hypothetical example illustrates the thrills and chills of margin investing. Margin requirements have been 50 percent for many years now. Thus, you can purchase $10,000 worth of stock for $5,000 of your own money, because the broker will lend you the rest. Brokers are delighted to lend you the money, because they charge you interest, often several points over the "broker call loan" rate, and the loan is collateralized, or secured, by the securities you purchase. When you buy 100 shares of X at $100 per share and send the broker just $5,000, you have leveraged your investment. Let's look at what can happen. Suppose the stock rises to $150 a share. You own the 100 shares, and they are now worth $15,000. You owe the broker the $5,000 he or she lent you, so your equity, or what's left over after deducting the amount you owe, is $10,000. Your stake, which started at $5,000, has doubled (before interest costs), while the stock has only risen 50 percent, all due to the magic of leverage. This is two-way magic, however. For suppose that the stock falls 50 percent instead to $50 a share. Then your shares are worth $5,000, exactly equal to what you owe the broker. Thus, your equity is now zero. A 50 percent decline in the stock price has wiped out your investment completely. Now of course the broker will not let this happen, because if the stock continued to drop, it would be worth less than the amount of the loan, and the broker could suffer a loss if you refused to honor your loan commitment. So he will warn you to take action before his capital is in jeopardy. By the time the stock has fallen to $75, your broker will ask you to either put up more cash or sell the stock. If you do not put up more cash, the brokerage house will sell the stock for you, to protect itself against a loss.

This "margin call," which many sage Wall Streeters say not to meet, can never occur if you never buy on margin, of course. A 25 percent decline in a stock is not unusual, and there is no reason for a PAD investor to panic. A margined investor will panic, however, when the broker begins hounding him for more money. It is quite common at the end of bear markets for many margin customers to have their accounts liquidated by brokers because they have insufficient equity. This wholesale dumping of stocks can feed on itself for a while, as prices continue to fall, forcing more margined stocks to be dumped. This is invariably an excellent time to be purchasing stocks for the long-term, and not on margin.

For decades, the Federal Reserve System has determined the margin rate for eligible securities. Although it has been at 50 percent for many years, there is now serious discussion of leaving the setting of margin requirements to the exchanges themselves, as part of financial deregulation. Without a doubt, the exchanges will set lower requirements to compete for business. A rate of 30–35 percent would not be surprising. Before the Great Crash margin requirements were 10 percent, and many investors were wiped out in the ensuing debacle. It could happen again.

RULE 4:   USE MARKET ORDERS ONLY.

Everyone loves a bargain. No one wants to pay list price. This holds true in the stock market, too. If you are ready to buy stock A at 22, and it drops to 21¼ and then returns to 22, it is a normal failing to think that you would rather pay 21¼ than 22. You may even be tempted to put in a "limit" order to purchase the stock when it reaches 21¾. I do not recommend this approach. When we take the long view, in which we expect the stock to rise to at least 44 (the 100 percent rule), it really does not make any difference whether we make the extra quarter point. It is also possible that the stock will not return to 21¾, and a large part of the upward movement could be sacrificed to gain a quarter of a point. I have made this mistake myself and am now sufficiently disciplined to use only "market" orders, to be executed at the market, and if this means paying 22⅛, so be it. Make up your mind, call your broker, execute your order, and hang up. Don't decide while you are on the telephone and the market is moving; it is only another short-run distraction.

Richard Ney, one of the modern muckrakers of Wall Street, has written an exposé of Wall Street's little-known exchange market makers, the specialists. I have no independent evidence that his accusations are true, but I have had my suspicions for a long time. The main thrust of his argument is that most specialists are interested first in making money for themselves, and only secondarily in making an orderly market in exchange-listed stocks, which is what they are supposed to do. One way they can profit at the expense of the public is through the entries in the specialist's "book," where all buy and sell orders, other than market orders, are entered. All of these limit or stop orders provide valuable information to the specialist, and uncommon opportunities. The details are in

Ney's book, which is listed at the end of the chapter. The exchanges piously deny any wrongdoing, which is of course self-serving. Don't make it any easier for the "Big Boys" to nail you.

B. SELLING: THE TOUGH DECISION

It is much easier to buy a stock than to sell it. In part, this reflects the basic optimism that infuses most of the investing public most of the time. In part, it also reflects the common mistake, which we have all made, of "falling in love" with a stock, thus losing the objectivity that is crucial to investment success. Selling decisions must be considered in an absolutely cold-blooded manner.

The two basic reasons for selling an individual stock, as opposed to a general selling program described in Chapter 4, are (1) to realize profits on a stock that has appreciated substantially, and (2) to eliminate stocks that have not performed up to expectations. Sales under (2) may result in either profits or losses. In the sections below I present the key rules to help you make the right selling decisions.

1. Selling a Stock that Has Performed Well

RULE 1:   SELL BETWEEN ONE-FOURTH AND ONE-HALF OF YOUR HOLDING WHEN IT HAS TRIPLED, AND THEN SELL ADDITIONAL FRACTIONS IF IT RISES SUBSTANTIALLY MORE. (USE STOCK SPLITS TO EASE THE PAIN OF PARTING.)

It is quite painful, and for some investors, impossible, to sell a stock that has been performing well. No one wants to miss the top, and mere mortals feel foolish when a stock continues to rise after it has been sold. Unfortunately, many stocks decline with the same vigor which accompanied a previous rise. The simplest solution to this dilemma is to establish rules for selling, and sell part of your position each time. Admittedly, no one can stick to all the rules all the time, but if you do not discipline yourself, you will be forfeiting a crucial PAD edge. I sell part of my holdings when a stock has tripled in price, and then pick further increments (I have often used 50 percent) to sell further parts. I find it particularly easy to follow Rule 1 when a stock has just split and I am in possession of some additional shares. This helps overcome the inertia and the sneaking suspicion that, in this one case, your tree will grow to the sky. It won't.

Rule 1 is also designed to prevent premature selling, which can destroy the PAD system. There will be losses, and perhaps large ones, but the big winners, if allowed to develop, will easily offset the losers. Although the PAD investor invests for the long term, this is appreciably shorter than forever. I cannot stress too much the twin dangers of selling after a stock

---

CASE HISTORY: GENERAL INSTRUMENT
(Figure 3.1)

I purchased General Instrument (NYSE-GRL) in 1975 at $4¼ per share (adjusted for a subsequent 3-for-1 stock split) and sold half of my position at $32 around split time. I was probably a little too patient in waiting for a stock split, since the price had already more than tripled long before. The stock then rose to a high of around $66, which should have triggered several sales, but I ignored my own rule. I sold the remainder in 1985 at 21¼, after GRL had underperformed the market for some time. This still resulted in a gain of 400 percent in 10 years.

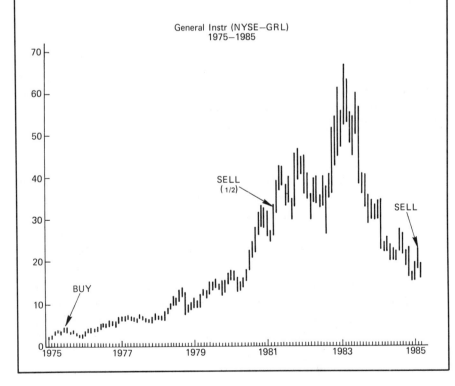

General Instr (NYSE—GRL)
1975—1985

has gone up a few points ("You can't go broke taking a profit") or refusing ever to sell until the big gains have all melted away. An intelligent but rarely followed adage is to cut your losses and let your profits run. Many investors do just the opposite, and pay dearly. (This type of investor behavior appears in many risky situations; see Chapter 7 for further details.) Obey the rules!

At some point it may be appropriate to liquidate all of your holdings in a particular stock. When a stock meets the criteria for a general selling program, as outlined in the next chapter, you may wish to sell all rather than part of your investment. I do not state this as a hard-and-fast rule, given that a stock you own could always be the next IBM and thus worth holding for a very long time even by PAD standards.

If your initial sale after a tripling is followed by a decline in price, you will feel very smart, unless you are still expecting perfection and thus upset that you did not sell it all. But you must steel yourself for the possibility that the stock will continue to rise even though you have correctly lightened your position. You must remind yourself that you have realized a very large profit, that you still own some of the stock, and that you do not need to buy at the bottom and sell at the top to get rich. What the rule really does is keep your greed under control. If you can do this successfully, and keep your fear under control too, your investment record will be enviable.

2. Selling a Stock that Has Not Performed Well

RULE 2:   IF A STOCK HAS DECLINED 50 PERCENT FROM PURCHASE PRICE, OR HAS PERFORMED SIGNIFICANTLY WORSE THAN THE MARKET FOR SIX MONTHS, OR HAS DROPPED TO A "5" FOR SHORT-TERM PERFORMANCE, IT MUST BE REEVALUATED CAREFULLY.

Mistakes are inevitable. Earnings fail to grow as anticipated, or the market places a lower value on those rising earnings. In either case, a stock, or perhaps several, becomes the black sheep in the family of investments, or to paraphrase Garrison Keillor, a dim bulb in your investment marquee. If you have called the market turn correctly and bought near the bottom, you may discover that some of your stocks do not rise as fast as the market; if your timing is somewhat less satisfactory, a market decline sends some of your stocks down at a precipitous rate. The question is when to get out and replace the dim bulbs. First, if you are a PAD investor, a price decline is a normal phase in the often inexplicable gyrations of the market and individual stocks. One should fully expect that a stock will decline after it is purchased, and it is a good rule to sit on a stock until it has declined 50 percent in price or has had at least two quarters of disappointing price action relative to the market before considering selling. I must emphasize that in neither case am I recommending a sale, just a thorough reexamination of the rationale for the purchase and the performance of the company since initial purchase. In addition, this rule does not have to be applied rigidly to stocks that have been in your portfolio for some time, but I recommend it, if only to prevent "falling in love" with a stock. This love is also blind, and will destroy the discipline of the PAD system.

One other event must trigger an immediate reevaluation of a stock: a drop in the Value Line short-term performance ranking to "5." This is a serious warning signal of hard times ahead, and they may be more than temporary.

Many investors and investment advisors argue strongly that stocks which decline in price by 10, 20, or 30 percent should be automatically eliminated from a portfolio. This is much too soon to bail out if you are a PAD investor, and these rules are among the most dubious of what passes for wisdom on Wall Street. Once your time horizon is measured in years, rather than weeks, a short-term decline can be suffered with equanimity. It may even present a better buying opportunity.

On the other hand, these 10–30 percent rules overlook those stocks which do not do well during an extended rally. These laggards need to be reevaluated, for fear they will collapse during the next market decline.

RULE 3: IF A STOCK REVIEWED UNDER RULE 2 SURVIVES A REEVALUATION, CASH RESERVES CAN BE COMMITTED TO IT. IF THE PRICE HAS FALLEN, THIS WILL ENABLE YOU TO "AVERAGE DOWN." THIS RULE SHOULD BE INVOKED ONLY ONCE FOR ANY STOCK AND DOES NOT APPLY TO A SHORT-TERM "5."

If the basic rationale for purchasing the stock still holds, and all that has happened is that the market has been weak, the price decline is an excellent opportunity to "average down," that is, buy some additional stock at a lower price. This is of course possible only if you still have some cash reserves. It is also a policy I would invoke only once, to avoid the risk of tying up too much capital in a stock that is not performing well, even if there is no apparent reason for the poor performance. Some stocks do go to zero, or close to it. You must avoid the paralyzing panic which prevents you from cutting your losses, and the easy and false rationalization, "It can't go any lower." It can. A $1 stock can still drop 100 percent.

Averaging down is not an option for a stock with a short-term performance ranking of "5." The only choice here is hold or sell. My decision in these kinds of cases is often influenced by the length of my Buy List. The longer it is, the more likely I am to try a "switch." (See Section B.5 below.)

RULE 4: DO NOT USE STOPLOSS ORDERS.

If you follow these rules, you obviously cannot use stoploss orders as they are generally prescribed on Wall Street. Stoploss orders set at 10–20 percent below purchase price (resulting in automatic sales) are inconsistent with a long-term strategy of investing in stocks that are fairly volatile. GRL is just one example of many: it declined to 2½ before starting its dramatic rise to $66. Those without patience and discipline walked out of the first act of a hit show.

RULE 5: USE MARKET ORDERS ONLY.

When the decision has been made to sell all or part of your holding in a particular stock, call up your discount broker and sell at the market. This is parallel advice to that given in the buying part of this chapter. It is not worth the time, effort, or risk to fight for quarters or eighths of a point.

RULE 6: SELL WHEN A MERGER OR BUYOUT IS ANNOUNCED.

In some happy circumstances, the market will help you decide when to sell. When another firm attempts a buyout or takeover of some kind, almost invariably at a price for your stock well above recent market prices, you have a golden opportunity to take your profits or cut your losses at a suddenly more favorable rate. Most high-technology companies that you will own will be taken over by companies in other industries, with less promising growth prospects. Fairchild Camera and Instrument, discussed in Chapter 2, is a perfect example.

My advice is to sell out and not even wait to receive the cash or stock from the deal. Some of the deals fall through, and since you don't want to own the stock of the acquiring company, don't wait. A possible exception to this rule could be made if the acquiring company is also a PAD high-technology company. It may be worthwhile to continue to hold stock in the combined company.

3. Reinvesting and Repurchasing

It is very difficult to get off a winning horse, although my rules listed above should help. But what to do with the proceeds of a sale? If your market timing analysis (Chapter 4) suggests that stocks will rise in the near future, I would pick one or more stocks from your Chapter 2 Buy List for reinvesting. If you already own the maximum number of stocks recommended for your portfolio size in Table 2.1, consider an additional investment in a stock you already own which still meets the PAD requirements. Otherwise hold cash reserves and wait for a better opportunity to buy.

Sometimes a previous winner that you have taken profits on, in accordance with the above rules, or completely liquidated, will again become attractive under the buying rules of Chapter 2. Do not hesitate to purchase it again. Similarly, a loser that was deleted from your portfolio should be considered in the future. Its management may change, or some R&D could begin to pay off, or a host of other factors could change. You may have just bought the stock a little too soon. The fact that you have been "burned" once is not a reason in itself to avoid a stock forever after.

RULE 7: REVIEW EVERY STOCK IN YOUR PORTFOLIO AT LEAST ONCE EVERY THREE MONTHS.*

All of your current holdings and prospective holdings should be reviewed regularly. I recommend at least once every quarter, which you can time with the regular reviews in the VLIS. As your portfolio gets larger, you may want to increase your time spent in review, but keep in mind that this is still just a serious hobby. You should guard against becoming too involved with either the market or your individual stocks. You must not lose your perspective.

---

*One of these four quarterly reviews should be the annual housecleaning discussed in Chapter 10 under Tax Strategy.

CASE HISTORY: ADVANCED MICRO DEVICES (NYSE-AMD)
(Figure 3.2)

I first bought AMD in 1981 at 7½. It performed poorly for some time after my purchase, and I sold it and took a tax loss in 1981 at 5⅞. I then repurchased the stock 31 days later at 5¾. The stock eventually rose above $40 a share. The graph shows my subsequent partial liquidations, all for handsome PAD profits. All of the selling was timed in accordance with the PAD rules—in particular, selling when additional stock is received. (All prices adjusted for 3-for-2 and 2-for-1 stock splits.)

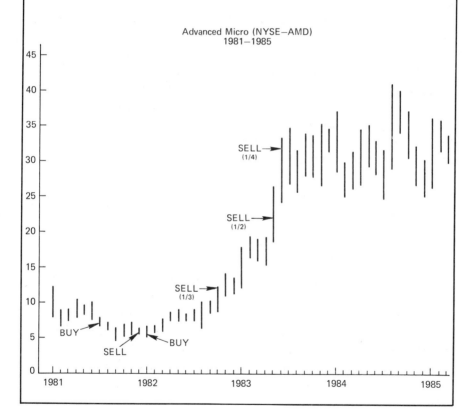

Advanced Micro (NYSE—AMD)
1981—1985

4. The Sell List

RULE 8: SELL STOCKS ON YOUR SELL LIST AT FIXED INTERVALS.

The rules presented in Sections 1–3 will produce a group of stocks which, for better or worse, are ready to be sold. Once a stock has been moved to this Sell List, do not wait for market timing indicators to signal "*sell.*" The stocks should be sold promptly, but I would recommend selling at fixed intervals if there is more than one stock on the Sell List, again to average out the unpredictable short-term fluctuations of the market. Selling one stock on your Sell List per week is a useful guideline.

If there are several stocks on your Sell List when the market timing indicators signal "*sell,*" you can begin selling promptly. If your Sell List does not contain any stocks at that time, however, it is necessary to build a Sell List from your current holdings. The easiest way to start this list is to review your entire portfolio for stocks that are far removed from qualifying for purchase. My favorite candidates are stocks whose Value Line 3–5 year appreciation potential, to the low end of the range, is zero or negative. Any stock rated "5" for short-term performance, which should already be under a cloud in your reviews, is also a good candidate for building a Sell List. I also look for stocks in my portfolio which have an appreciation potential to the high end of the range of less than 100 percent. Any stock that has dropped below minimum acceptable R&D spending, or minimum financial strength or safety ratings, is also a prime candidate for the Sell List. This set of criteria will almost surely be enough to generate a sizable Sell List. Since market timing indicators are signaling falling prices, all of the proceeds should be placed in cash reserves after a general selling program. While I have established no maximum level of cash reserves, I believe a PAD investor should be willing to keep as much as 50 percent of a portfolio in cash. This should ease the pain of any decline, provide the funds to capitalize on a decline, and yet allow participation in an unexpected bull market. (Certain options strategies can provide further insurance against market declines, and these are discussed in Chapter 9.)

5. Switching

It is not at all unusual for some stocks to be added to your Buy List at the same time that other stocks in your portfolio are being added to your Sell List. If the market timing indicators are either neutral or bullish, you can execute a switch, in which you sell a Sell List stock and immediately reinvest the proceeds in a Buy List stock. This kind of portfolio upgrading can be overdone, of course, and just result in high commissions and loss of patience and discipline. But when stocks have appeared on both your lists, and you have no reason not to be fully invested, make the switches. It is probably less difficult to sell a stock, particularly one you have held a long time, if you have a replacement waiting in the wings. Also, I am more willing to move those stocks which have fallen to "5" for short-term performance to the Sell List if I have stocks on the Buy List ready to substitute for them.

SUMMARY OF RULES FOR THIS CHAPTER

Buying

1. Use a discount broker exclusively.
2. Buy stocks on your Buy List at fixed intervals.
3. Do not buy on margin.
4. Use market orders only.

Selling

1. Sell between one-fourth and one-half of your holding when it has tripled, and then sell additional fractions if it rises substantially more. (Use stock splits to ease the pain of parting.)
2. If a stock has declined 50 percent from purchase price, or has performed significantly worse than the market for six months, or has dropped to a "5" for short-term performance, it must be reevaluated carefully.
3. If a stock reviewed under Rule 2 survives a reevaluation, cash reserves can be committed to it. If the price has fallen, this will enable you to "average down." This rule should be invoked only once for any stock and does not apply to a short-term "5."
4. Do not use stoploss orders.
5. Use market orders only.
6. Sell when a merger or buyout is announced.

7. Review every stock in your portfolio at least once every three months.

8. Sell stocks on your Sell List at fixed intervals.

Readings for the PAD Investor

Winning: The Psychology of Successful Investing. By Srully Blotnick. Published by McGraw-Hill, New York 1979. Chapter 5, "Stockbrokers," should convince you to use a discount broker. Overall, the book is an interesting study of investing from the psychological viewpoint.

The Wall Street Jungle. By Richard Ney. Published by Grove Press, New York 1970. If you want to believe the wheel is crooked, this is the book for you. At the very least, Ney should convince you not to use limit orders of any kind.

APPENDIX: DISCOUNT BROKERS—WHAT TO LOOK FOR

As a PAD investor you will do your own research and make your own decisions about stock purchases and sales. Thus, there is no need to pay a full-service broker for research and advice that you do not and should not use. Discount brokers provide brokerage services without the research and advice and pass the cost savings on to their customers. Table 3.A.1, located at the end of this appendix, contains a sampling of discounters large and small.*

      I use three criteria for selecting a discount broker: *cost, service,* and *safety.* Each of these is discussed below.

A. COST

The main reason to use a discount broker is to save money on commissions. These savings are substantial, even with the relatively infrequent trades of a PAD investor. For example, purchase of 300 shares of a $20 stock may easily cost more than $100 at a full-service brokerage firm, while even the most expensive discounters will charge about $70, and the least expensive discounters may charge as little as $26. It seems almost sinful

---

*The list is by no means exhaustive nor does inclusion on the list or exclusion from it imply anything about the desirability of dealing with any firm.

that PAD investors can save hundreds of dollars a year without giving up anything!

Unfortunately, it is not possible to rate discounters by cost. Each firm has its own system for calculating commissions, and these commission schedules can change at any time. Some firms charge by value of transaction, some by number of shares, some by both. All have minimum charges which may apply to a transaction. Thus, some orders will be cheapest to execute at one firm, and others will be cheapest at another firm. While you could set up accounts at many firms and execute each of your orders at the cheapest possible price, it will be much less time consuming to pick one firm that is cheap for you: examine your recent transactions and then compare what your total commissions would be at several of the discounters listed in Table 3.A.1, or any other firms you wish to consider. Several will no doubt come out below the others. You may want to choose among the leaders on the basis of service (Section B), or safety (Section C). If you are dissatisfied with your first choice, you can switch to another fairly painlessly. I have switched several times in search of the optimal combination of low rates and good service. I like to shop around every few years just to make sure I cannot do better elsewhere.

All discounters should be willing to provide you with commission schedules to do your calculations. One toll-free telephone call will also get you account forms, lists of other services, and a recent financial statement. PAD investors following Rule 1 of Chapter 3 on page 37, will often be selling round lots combined with odd lots. It is worth checking the commission schedules carefully to determine just how expensive a combination trade is. Some firms may charge as much for the odd lot as for the round lot, while others may add on only a nominal amount to the round-lot charge.

B. SERVICE

Low commissions will not be a bargain if you cannot get through to your broker quickly, get rapid executions of your orders, and get prompt confirmations of your trades. Discounters vary in the quality of this basic and most important service. If you have trusted friends with discount brokerage accounts, they should be able to tell you just how good the basic service is at their discounter. Otherwise, you must find out through a process of trial and error. Remember, though, that you need not put up with unsatisfactory service. Complain. If that fails, open an account with another discounter. There are plenty of fish in the sea.

Several other aspects of service may be important to you. For example, I will not tolerate brusqueness on the telephone. I also expect to get monthly statements that are easy to understand, complete, and correct. I also look for interest paid on balances awaiting reinvestment, prompt payment of balances, and delivery of securities. You may wish to add other criteria to this list. Search until you find them.

Many discounters offer services formerly available only at full-service brokerage firms: cash-management accounts, mutual funds, IRAs and Keoghs, and many more. If these services are important to you, and it simplifies your life to have all your financial dealings with one firm, go ahead and use them. These services are not necessarily free, however, and some of their costs may be included in commission rates.

Some discounters have established networks of offices throughout the United States. I consider this to be a dubious advantage. There is no reason for a PAD investor to visit a discount brokerage office. It is safer to deal only over the telephone, and use the mail. This approach reduces the risk of getting too close to Wall Street.

C. SAFETY

The failure of Brevill, Bressler, and Schulman was an important reminder of the fragility of our financial intermediaries. No discount brokerage customers lost any money in this failure, however. The firm's accounts were taken over by another brokerage firm soon after the failure. Yet this failure was no doubt a jolt to customers of discount brokers everywhere. How can we be sure our assets are safe?

Our main protection is the Securities Investor Protection Corporation (SIPC) which insures most brokerage accounts up to $500,000. Some discount brokers have additional protection up to $2,500,000. Even with SIPC protection, investors still may have their capital or securities tied up for some time in the unlikely event of a failure. The best way to reduce this risk is to take delivery of your securities, and keep your cash balances in a money market mutual fund. Examining a financial statement may provide some additional confidence, and dealing with one of the larger discounters may also help. Several are subsidiaries of the nation's largest banks, which may also inspire confidence.

D. SUMMARY

Find the discount brokerage that meets your own requirements best, and then use them and save. When you discover that another firm can do a better job, switch. PAD investors should get top value for their commission dollars.

TABLE 3.A.1   A Sampling of Discount Brokerages

Burke, Christensen & Lewis 120 South LaSalle Streeet Chicago, IL 60603 Telephone: 1–800–621–0392	A regional discounter with offices in the Midwest, BCL has one of the lower rates for 100 shares ($25) but is not as cheap for 300 share orders.
Fidelity Brokerage Services Priority Mail Center 400 E. Las Colinas Blvd. PO Box 660603 Dallas, TX 75266 Telephone: 1–800–544–6666	FBS is part of the Fidelity network, which includes Fidelity mutual funds. Minimum commission is $33. Not one of the lowest priced, but has many services and is large.
Heartland Securities 208 South LaSalle Street Chicago, IL 60604 Telephone: 1–800–621–0662	This Midwestern discounter probably has the lowest rates for odd lots. Maximum commission is $15+15 cents per share. A 100-share order will cost $30, but a 20-share order will cost only $18, which may be the lowest price in the industry.
Ovest Financial Services 90 Broad Street New York, NY 10004 Telephone: 1–800–255–0700	Relatively low-priced discounter with even lower commissions for active traders, who are not PAD investors!
Pacific Brokerage Services 5757 Wilshire Boulevard Los Angeles, CA 90036 Telephone: 1–800–421–8395	PBS charges $26 for 100, 200, or 300 shares and $28 for odd lots or round lots combined with odd lots. One of the least expensive in the 100–500 share range.
Quick & Reilly 120 Wall Street New York, NY 10005 Telephone: 1–800–672–7220	One of the largest discounters with a nationwide network of offices. Minimum commission is $35. One of the more expensive firms, but it offers many services.
Robinson Securities 11 South LaSalle Street Chicago, IL 60603 Telephone: 1–800–621–2840	Robinson has a low $22.50 minimum commission, and a $25 maximum for 100 shares.

Rose and Company
One Financial Place
Chicago, IL 60605
Telephone: 1–800–435–4000

Rose is a division of Chase Manhattan. Customers get access to Chase financial services, and enjoy the backing of a large bank, but must pay relatively high discount commissions.

Charles Schwab
1722 "I" Street
Washington, DC 20006
Telephone: 1–800–553–5000

One of the largest discounters, Schwab is a subsidiary of BankAmerica. You get size and safety, but you must pay high discount commissions.

Muriel Siebert & Co.
444 Madison Avenue
New York, NY 10022
Telephone: 1–800–872–0711

Siebert charges a $30 minimum, and has commissions well under the most expensive discounters.

Note: All information was collected in May, 1986, from sources believed to be reliable, but it cannot be guaranteed. Discount brokers may change their rate schedules frequently, and also change headquarters locations and telephone numbers. The *Wall Street Journal* and the *New York Times* are good places to look for up-to-date advertisements of discounters.

4

MARKET TIMING

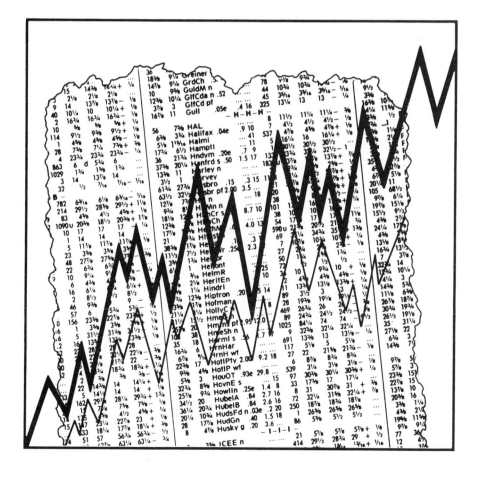

"How's the market today?" This question must be asked millions of times each day between the hours of 9:30 a.m. and 4 p.m. Eastern Time. Yet no one owns the market. As a stockbroker I once knew used to say, "It's a market of stocks, not a stock market." But this idea is dangerously misleading, because when the market goes down, so will most of your stocks, most of the time, even if there is no reason. Wall Street commentators are paid regular salaries to tell audiences why the market went up or down on a particular day, but I am firmly convinced that no one knows, and that it does not matter. The fluctuations do matter, however, as great PAD stocks bought at the beginning of a bear market will fall—probably a lot—even if their long term prospects are still bright. A disciplined investor can avoid buying at market tops and can concentrate purchases during periods of undervaluation and sales during periods of overvaluation. This rare ability can be cultivated with a combination of fundamental, technical, and psychological indicators of the market's likely overall direction. Market timing rules, in combination with the stock selection rules of Chapter 2, are the twin beacons that will guide the PAD investor to financial success.

A. THE FUNDAMENTAL APPROACH

RULE 1: THE MARKET IS OK TO BUY IF VALUE LINE INVEST-
MENT SURVEY MEDIAN APPRECIATION POTENTIAL EQUALS OR
EXCEEDS 100 PERCENT. SELLING SHOULD BE UNDERTAKEN WHEN
THIS POTENTIAL IS BELOW 75 PERCENT. 75–95 PERCENT IS A
NEUTRAL AREA.

The most important question to be asked about the market, in a fundamental sense, is how fairly is it valued compared to historical norms?
The valuation that is crucial, however, is not price relative to current earnings, but price relative to future earnings capitalized at historical norms.
The best single measure of overvaluation or undervaluation is published
by Value Line: the median estimated appreciation potential (MAP) for
all 1,700 stocks followed by the service (Figure 4.1, line A). This median
has fluctuated between 234 percent at the bottom of the 1974 bear market,
perhaps the worst postwar market debacle, and 18 percent at the market
peak in 1968, one of the most severe periods of overvaluation in modern
times. My rule of thumb is that if this median is at least 100 percent, the
market is not overvalued and it is OK to buy. Once this indicator falls
below 100 percent, it is time to be cautious. I consider 75–95 percent to
be a neutral range: delay any new investments until the MAP is more
favorable. (Switching is still OK.) When the MAP falls below 75 percent,
begin to build cash reserves by selling stocks. Chapters 2 and 3 will guide
you in making up your Sell List.

In recent years, this indicator has been a good timing guide for a
PAD investor. In the last stage of the 1982–83 bull market, for example,
the MAP fell as low as 55 percent, which was a definite warning sign of
the 1984 bear market. In the summer of 1984, which was a good time
to buy stocks, the MAP was again over 100 percent. By the time the Dow
had pierced 1300 in 1985, the MAP had fallen back to the neutral range,
and it fell to the sell range after the Dow Jones soared past 1500 at the
end of 1985. Note that the MAP may have an unusually large change in
the July–August period, simply because Value Line extends its 3–5 year
forecasts for individual stocks by one calendar year at that time.

While this rule is the only fundamental one I list in this chapter, it
is probably as valuable as any other rule in the book. It provides a fairly
objective indication of the state of the market compared to historical norms,
a priceless long-term perspective.

B. THE TECHNICAL APPROACH

Stock exchange trading generates an enormous supply of data every day. All of the prices, volumes, and the like can be analyzed in an almost infinite variety of ways in an attempt to foresee market trends. Those who study the data are called market technicians, and what they create are technical indicators whose levels or changes give advance warning of market rallies and declines. Some are of course more reliable than others, yet I do not consider any one indicator sufficiently reliable to let it determine my investment posture. But a collection of ten indicators, called the Wall Street Week Technical Market Index, has had such an enviable forecasting record in recent years that it should be monitored by PAD investors. I discuss this index and its use below, and then list individual technical indicators that can signal market bottoms and tops with some degree of reliability. My favorites are marked (F). (A PAD investor with limited time can simply monitor rules 1 and 2.)

1. The "Wall Street Week" Technical Market Index (WSW TMI)

RULE 2:   DO NOT COMMENCE A BUYING PROGRAM UNDER RULE 1 IF THE "WALL STREET WEEK" TECHNICAL MARKET INDEX HAS A SELL SIGNAL IN EFFECT.

This index was created for the PBS television program, "Wall Street Week." It is announced every Friday near the beginning of the program. As I noted above, its recent forecasting record is outstanding: the Index correctly gave buy signals in the summer of 1982, and a sell signal in the summer of 1983. It then gave a well-timed buy signal in May, 1984, which was in effect through July 1986.

The TMI is composed of ten technical indicators, none of which is sufficiently reliable by itself to signal market turns. Each individual indicator is rated as bullish, bearish, or neutral, and the Index itself does not give a buy signal until there are at least five more bullish indicators than there are bearish ones, ignoring the neutrals. The reverse is true for a sell signal, that is, there must be at least five more bearish indicators than there are bullish ones, and any signal is in effect until the opposite one is given. The Index can be used to improve Rule 1 purchase timing: even if the market is "OK to buy" under Rule 1, it may not be near a bottom.

THE VALUE LINE Investment Survey

Part 1
Summary
&
Index

August 9, 1985

File at the front of the Ratings & Reports binder. Last week's Summary & Index should be removed.

TABLE OF SUMMARY-INDEX CONTENTS

The Median of Estimated
PRICE-EARNINGS RATIOS
of all stocks with earnings

12.1

26 Weeks Ago*	Market Low 12-23-74*	Market High 12-13-68*
11.2	4.8	19.0

The Median of
ESTIMATED YIELDS
(next 12 months) of all dividend
paying stocks under review

3.3%

26 Weeks Ago*	Market Low 12-23-74*	Market High 12-13-68*
3.4%	7.8%	2.7%

The Estimated Median
APPRECIATION POTENTIAL
of all 1700 stocks in the hypothesized
Economic environment 3 to 5 years hence

80%

A

26 Weeks Ago*	Market Low 12-23-74*	Market High 12-13-68*
85%	234%	18%

*Estimated medians as published in The Value Line Investment Survey on the dates shown.

Figure 4.1

ANALYSES OF INDUSTRIES IN ALPHABETICAL ORDER WITH PAGE NUMBER

Numeral in parenthesis after the industry is rank for probable performance (next 12 months).

Industry	PAGE	Industry	PAGE	Industry	PAGE	Industry	PAGE
Advertising (73)	1816	Computer Software & Serv.(44)	2104	Insurance-Diversified (38)	2062	Petroleum-Integrated (50)	401
Aerospace/Defense (24)	551	Copper (82)	1215	Insurance-Life (18)	1194	Petroleum-Producing (77)	1824
Agric. Equip./Diversified (90)	1431	Distilling/Tobacco (20)	337	Insurance-Prop./Cas. (69)	631	Precision Instrument (62)	150
Air Transport (9)	1739, 251	Drug Industry (10)	1247	Investment Company (39)	2082	Publishing (12)	1785
Aluminum (64)	1215	Drugstore (30)	786	Iron Ore (78)	1215	Railroad/Resources (40)	308
Apparel (52)	1601	*Electrical Equipment (54)	1001	Lead, Zinc & Minor Mtls. (59)	619	Real Estate (41)	672
Auto & Truck (35)	101	Electric Utility-Cent. (31)	701	Machinery (65)	1301	REIT (25)	667,1167
Auto Parts-OEM (63)	802	Electric Utility-East (29)	177	Machinery-Const. (48)	1358	Recreation (42)	1751
Auto Parts-Replacement (84)	112	Electric Utility-West (45)	1718	Machine Tool (70)	1344	Restaurant (23)	319
Bank (2)	2001	*Electronics (89)	1032	Manu.Housing/Rec. Veh. (60)	1554	Retail-Special Lines (57)	1694
Bank (Midwest) (28)	645	European Diversified (32)	826	Maritime (88)	294	Retail Store (13)	1640
Bank (Southwest) (56)	659	Financial Services (5)	2046	Medical Services (4)	1270	Savings & Loan (6)	1151
Brewing/Soft Drink (36)	1542	Food Processing (22)	1451	Medical Supplies (16)	213	Securities Brokerage (17)	1184
Broadcasting/Cable TV (7)	371	Food Wholesalers (8)	1532	Metal Fabricating (47)	585	Shoe (76)	1681
Building (46)	851	Foreign Stocks (Japanese)(58)	1565	Metals & Mining-Gen'l (86)	1215	Steel-General (21)	606
Building Supplies (55)	896	Furn./Home Furnishings(49)	914	Multiform (51)	1376	Steel-Integrated (74)	989,1419
Canadian Energy (66)	434	Gold/Diamond (S.A.) (—)	1206	Natural Gas (Diversified)(91)	450	Steel-Specialty (80)	2098
Cement (67)	904	Gold (No. American) (83)	1215	Natural Gas (Utility)(71)	476	Telecommunications (53)	751
Chemical-Basic (37)	1237	Grocery (14)	1505	Newspaper (1)	1807	Textile (85)	1624
Chemical-Diversified (68)	1886	Home Appliance (33)	137	*Office Equip.&Suppls (19)	137	Tire & Rubber (72)	125
Chemical-Specialty (34)	508	Hotel/Gaming (27)	1770	Oilfield Services (87)	1841	Toiletries/Cosmetics (26)	811
Coal/Uran./Geothermal (75)	1874	Household Products (79)	975	Packaging & Cont. (15)	956	Toys & School Supplies (3)	795
Comp. and Peripherals (81)	1083	Industrial Services (11)	348	Paper & Forest Prods. (61)	926	Trucking/Trans Lease (43)	278

*Reviewed in this week's edition.

In three parts: This is Part I, the Summary & Index. Part II is Selection & Opinion. Part III is Ratings & Reports. Volume XL, No. 46.

Published weekly by VALUE LINE, INC. 711 Third Avenue, New York, N.Y. 10017
For the confidential use of subscribers. Reprint by permission only. Copyright 1985 by Value Line, Inc.

Figure 4.1 (*continued*)

(Copyright 1985, Value Line, Inc.
Reprinted with permission.)

To avoid getting in too soon, do not commit cash reserves if a WSW TMI sell signal is in effect. The reverse is not true, however. If Rule 1 signals "*sell*," you should sell even if WSW TMI is bullish. It does not pay to stay to the end of a bull market. Leave the party before it's over.

3. Technical Indicators of Market Bottoms

a. New lows (F)

Every day all major newspapers report in their financial sections the number of NYSE stocks that traded, on the previous day, at their lowest price in the past 52 weeks. These are called new lows. When the number of new lows exceeds 400 in a day, it is usually a sign that the market is nearing an important bottom and will begin rising soon. It takes a large amount of general selling pressure to drive 400 stocks to new 52-week lows in one day, and this is usually a sign of, and also a cause of, great pessimism on Wall Street. Many margin accounts are also damaged in this kind of selling, which can bring on further liquidation.

The indicator is not always reliable, however, partly because the definition of "new low" has changed in recent years. Under the old system, price records were kept on a calendar-year basis, so a new low in April was only a four-month new low price, for example. Only between December and March were new lows really low prices for a year. Now, in the computer age, prices are always compared with the previous 52-week range. In 1982 and 1984, new lows never reached the 400 + level even at market bottoms.

b. Oddlot sales-to-purchases ratio

Oddlotters, those who trade fewer than 100 shares (a round lot) at a time have a time-honored reputation for being wrong at critical market turning points. This reputation is rather self-serving, for the Wall Street community in general is often wrong about the market. Nonetheless, the intensity of oddlot selling compared to buying tends to pick up at market bottoms. A good rule of thumb here is that when this ratio of shares sold to shares bought reaches 3.0, the "little guy," as he is condescendingly known on Wall Street, is getting panicky and the market is approaching a bottom.

The sale/purchase indicator often shows the effects of forced liquidation of stock from margin accounts in the final stages of a bear market. The patient investor can profit from the bargain basement prices if he avoids buying on margin and can keep from being swept along with the lemmings marching to the sea. This is of course very difficult to do. The herd instinct is very strong, and the managers of billions of dollars are subject to the same human frailties as ordinary investors. (The importance of psychology in market timing is discussed in Section C below.)

During the summer of 1984, the sale/purchase ratio exceeded 3.0, which is an unusually high level. In the summer of 1985, with the Dow-Jones Industrial Average 250 points above its 1984 low, the sale/purchase ratio fell to a neutral range between 2 and 2.5, but again returned to 3 before the market rallied sharply in 1985.

c. CBOE put-volume/call-volume ratio (F)

Chapter 9 is devoted entirely to the explanation of options trading and options strategies for the PAD investor. I include here only the briefest summary explanation of one kind of option, to make this technical indicator a little less abstruse.

A call option gives the buyer the right to buy a stock from the option writer at a specified price for a certain period of time. A put option gives the buyer the right to sell a stock to the option writer at a specified price for a certain period of time. A put buyer is betting on or hedging against a decline in a particular stock, while a call buyer is betting on or hedging against a rise in a particular stock. Thus, put buyers are bearish and call buyers bullish. Some options traders buy or sell combinations of puts and/or calls, but their activity will have a smaller effect on the volume ratio.

Trading in these options has mushroomed in the past decade, with the creation of organized exchanges to trade options on many stocks. The oldest and largest is the Chicago Board Options Exchange (CBOE). The *Wall Street Journal,* the *New York Times,* and various financial publications carry complete listings of daily options trading.* The number of puts and calls purchased each day varies fairly regularly with the market's short-term trend. Normally, call volume exceeds put volume by a significant amount, as option buyers tend to be (over?) optimistic. When the ratio of CBOE put volume to call volume exceeds .9, it is quite likely the market is making a short-term bottom. The higher the ratio, the more powerful the ensuing rally should be. The buyers of puts and calls are supposed to be, in the aggregate, relatively uninformed investors who run with the herd that the PAD investor is trying to avoid. Although this ratio

---

*See Chapter 9 for an example of a daily options trading report.

falls significantly during a bull market, and can stay as low as .3, it does not signal tops as reliably as bottoms. I would consider persistent readings below .4 to be grounds for caution, however.

The put-volume/call-volume ratio does have an excellent short-term forecasting record, which is partially documented in Figures 4.2 and 4.3.

d. Volume and the selling climax

Often, in the last stage of a bear market, there is a final precipitous drop of stock prices accompanied by very high volume. This collapse is usually followed immediately, even in the same day, by an upsurge of equal or even greater violence. You have not earned your investing stripes until you have survived one of these "selling climaxes." Unfortunately, not all bear markets end this way. Many die with a whimper rather than a bang. The 1981–82 bear market is a case in point. The last day of decline in August before one of the greatest rallies in postwar history saw the Dow-Jones Average fall by a minuscule 0.08 points. Complete exhaustion, but no climax. An investor waiting for a selling climax would have missed the entire 1982–83 bull market. In general, I think volume is a dubious indicator of any market trend, either up or down.

e. Mutual fund cash percentage

The "big guy" can be wrong, too. Mutual fund managers often accumulate cash reserves as the market declines, and these reserves reach a peak at market bottoms. At market tops, cash reserves are often extremely small. Let this pattern be a caution to those who will trust all their money to mutual fund managers. Let it also be an indicator for the PAD investor: when the cash percentage is 15 percent or greater, stocks are probably ready for a significant rally. The statistic is regularly mentioned on the market commentary page of the *Wall Street Journal,* which is how I keep current on it.

The major drawback of this indicator is that there is some controversy about the correct measurement of the cash percentage. The problem is that some mutual fund managers may stash their cash in treasury notes, for example. These are highly liquid and can be sold in an instant to buy stocks, but they may not be counted as cash. You can follow the controversy on the market commentary page of the *Wall Street Journal.*

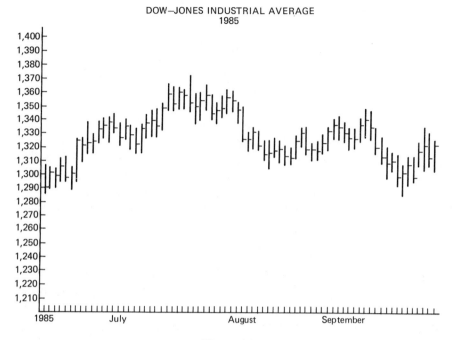

Figure 4.2

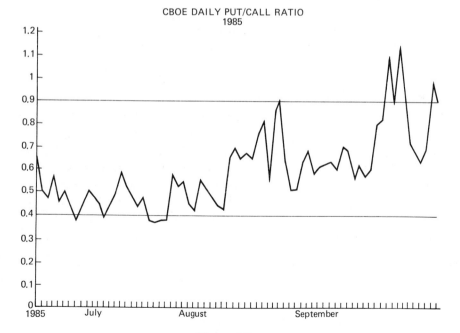

Figure 4.3

f. Investor's Intelligence™ Sentiment Index

Investor's Intelligence is an investment advisory letter which compiles
an index of the sentiment of over 100 market letters, and its success as
a contrary indicator should give pause to anyone who subscribes to a large
number of market letters. Advisory letters tend to be bullish most of the
time, probably reflecting the tendency of their readers to be bullish most
of the time. When a large minority, or a majority of letters are bearish,
this usually signifies enough pessimism for a market bottom. Extremes
of optimism, in which very few letters are bearish relative to historical
norms, usually signal a market top. Rating the letters for bullish or bearish
is as much an art as a science, though. This index is proprietary, and
therefore not free, but it has a good track record as a contrary indicator.

g. Indicators old and new

Two indicators publicized in 1984 in the *Wall Street Journal* are the
Greed Index, compiled by Lee H. Idleman,* and the Diaper Index,
compiled by John Mendelson.† Both are designed to measure fear and
greed on Wall Street. While the published report does not provide much
support for the accuracy of the Diaper Index, the Greed Index may be
a useful indicator. Again, since it is proprietary, one either pays the price
or waits to read about it in the *Wall Street Journal*.

Two other well-known indicators are the GM indicator and the Dow
Theory. I feel these both have limited usefulness, although their proponents
obviously think otherwise. *Caveat emptor.* The GM indicator stakes
everything on the movement of the price of GM stock. In general, when
GM stock is in an uptrend, that is good for the market, and when it is
in a downtrend, that is bad for the market. GM usually moves with the
market, but in those instances where it does not, I cannot see any reason
why it can predict a change of direction for the entire market. When GM
is at its peak (or nadir), so is the market much of the time. Indeed, there
is even controversy here, with proponents of this indicator disagreeing,
in the *Wall Street Journal*, on the timing of true buy and sell signals.‡

The Dow Theory, another old indicator, uses the Dow-Jones
Transportation Average to confirm any signals given by the Dow-Jones

---

*See the *Wall Street Journal*, May 29, 1984.

†See the *Wall Street Journal*, May 25, 1984.

‡See the *Wall Street Journal*, October 18, 1984.

Industrial Average, such as a decline below a previous major low (bearish), or a rise above a previous major peak (bullish). When the Transports fail to perform in the same manner, the original signal is not confirmed. It seems to me that by the time the signal finally is confirmed, the bear or bull market could be closer to its end than its beginning. It certainly tells us nothing about market turning points, which is the primary goal of market timing of any type.

h. Others yet unborn

There are many other technical indicators of the market's current condition and future health. As we have seen, the *Wall Street Journal*, especially the market commentary page, is a good source of information on new indicators. New indicators are probably being created at least as fast as old ones are being retired from the Wall Street battlefield. A good reference source, which should give any reader sufficient amounts of technical analysis to last a lifetime, is contained in a Chartcraft, Inc. publication called the *Encyclopedia of Stock Market Techniques*. It even has supplements, which will keep you up to date on the creation of new indicators. If you find an indicator that works, use it. But if there is no basis for its accuracy, I would be quite cautious. It is well-known that the numbers of strikeouts of the old Washington Senators baseball team tracked the market very well for a number of years. And then there is the Superbowl indicator. While I can't deny that this indicator has a good predictive record, and was right on target in 1985 and 1986, do we really want to bet our investment dollars on the outcome of a football game? I do not, but I must admit that it seems that many others do. The rally on the Monday after the 1985 Superbowl was quite impressive. If enough Wall Streeters rely on this indicator, it could work for some time just because it is believed to work. This is of course a self-fulfilling prophecy, and a dangerous one.

If you are intrigued by this indicator, it should be noted that the Superbowl "theory" is silent on the effects on the market of a victory by an expansion team that was neither in the old AFL (bearish for the market for that year) or the old NFL (bullish for the market for that year). Note also that there are four old NFL teams in the AFC, so it is possible to have a Superbowl contest between two old NFL teams. In this case, if enough investors believe the indicator, the market should rally before the Superbowl is even played!

2. Technical Indicators of Market Tops

The preceding indicators are generally better at signaling market bottoms rather than tops, with the exception of "Wall Street Week's" elves, which do both well. The following ones may be of some help in pinpointing market tops. Again, my favorites are marked (F).

a. New highs

Although the number of 52-week new highs is not as reliable as the number of new lows, massive numbers of new highs, say 400 or more, are a signal for caution. The optimism generated by this pleasant turn of events will feed on itself for a time, but eventually we return to earth.

b. Bad breadth

Many technicians study the number of stocks advancing each day relative to the number declining, called market breadth, and add or subtract the difference to a cumulative total which, when plotted on graph paper, is called the advance-decline (A/D) line. While I would not put too much faith in the squiggles of the A/D line, there is a fundamental truth here: When the market is advancing, it frequently happens that it will get tired, that is, fewer and fewer stocks will participate in the uptrend by closing higher for the day. Breadth gets bad. This period of "brutal selectivity" often characterizes the last stage of a bull market. Fewer than 1,000 advancing stocks on an up day is often a short-term sign that the market is getting tired. Unfortunately, it can happen that the market can "catch its breadth" and start rising again. A PAD investor needs more than breadth to be moved to buy or sell stock.

A/D technicians also use the term "divergence" to mean that the A/D line is not moving in tandem with the popular market averages. When the A/D line lags behind the averages in a rally, this is negative divergence and should indicate that the rally will not continue. Divergence in the opposite direction may signal the end of a market decline. Again, the main value of this indicator is as a check on the popular averages.

Another form of divergence occurs when the popular averages do not move in tandem to new highs in a bull market. This divergence is also supposed to be unhealthy for the market. A recent example of this form of divergence occurred in 1985, when the rise in General Foods stock caused the Dow-Jones Average to make new highs when the rest of the market averages did not. The market then proceeded to rally strongly. Remember this example the next time you are told about the evils of divergence.

c. The *Time Magazine* indicator (F)

This used to be my favorite indicator, in part because I never liked the magazine much (they never published my letters) and in part because I thought no one else knew about it. There is very little new under the sun on Wall Street, however, as this indicator has been mentioned in the *Wall Street Journal*.

Time Magazine has a record for predicting the stock market and the fortunes of individual companies that is second to just about everyone. A favorable story about a company should be treated the same as the *Sports Illustrated* cover story jinx (same publishing company!). When *Time* runs an upbeat story on the market, it's time to build cash reserves. When *Time* features a stock of yours that has had a major runup, it is time to sell. I know. It first happened to me in 1975, which is when I discovered this indicator. I held Fairchild Camera and Instrument, which in the beginning of 1975 had a meteoric rise mentioned in the July 7 issue of *Time Magazine*. This was, of course, its peak price for several years. The price chart of Fairchild in Chapter 2 shows the approximate date of the *Time* story and the price level at that time. After Fairchild's price collapse, I did some further research. I remembered that *Time* had featured McDonald's on its cover in September, 1973. Sure enough, the stock fell by more than 70 percent in 14 months, as shown in Figure 4.4.

I have resisted purchasing IBM stock, even if it meets all of the criteria of Chapter 2, because *Time* ran a cover story on "Big Blue" in July, 1983. This was sufficient to convince me that everyone's favorite would be a dog for some time to come. Hard times, by IBM's standards, did arrive, and the stock did not do well for years after the cover story (Figure 4.5.)

In the summer of 1985, *Time* devoted a full-page story to the improving fortunes of Cray Research, one of the few high-technology stocks that doubled in 1985. I sold some of my holdings even though the stock had not quite tripled from my purchase price, just to be on the safe side.

The *Time* magazine indicator is not like the Superbowl indicator at all. *Time* is rarely a first source for news of any kind. Most of the stories are already old news by the time they are reported. If a company has built up a growth record enviable enough to be reported in detail in *Time*, it is probably ripe for a fall from grace. When the market has advanced or declined strongly enough to be chronicled in *Time*, the movement is probably over. I would consider a cover story on a raging bull market to be a major sell signal. Likewise, a cover story on a raging bear market would be a major buy signal. (This indicator is not perfect, however. I found a January, 1955 cover story on a bull market which did not appear at the peak.)

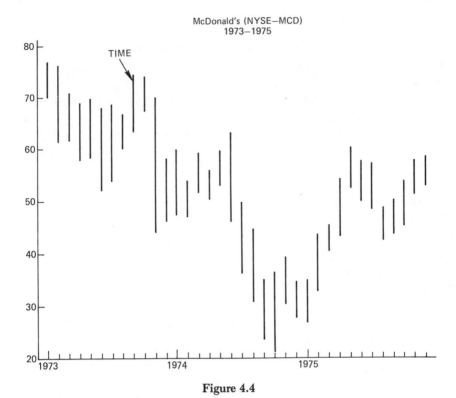

Figure 4.4

d. Speculative excesses in new issues (IPOs) (F)

Often in the final phase of a bull market, relatively unseasoned speculative stocks, especially initial public offerings (IPOs) or new issues, outperform the general market by a wide margin. This is one indication of a frenzy that is invariably followed by disappointment. A large volume of new issues is sufficient cause for alarm, although I have no quantitative measure for it. A rapid rise in the NASDAQ index, which consists of many speculative issues, is another warning sign. The most dangerous sign of impending doom can often be found in the pages of the *Wall Street Journal*. In February, 1983, when the stock of Diasonics went public, it was reported that a number of buyers of the stock had not the slightest idea of their business, other than that it was "hot." These "investors" pushed the price from $22 a share on the offering to $29 before the roof fell in. The stock subsequently fell as low as $2, and recovered to just $4 while the Dow was soaring past 1500. The entire OTC market began a severe decline shortly after Diasonics reached its peak price. There will be new issues crazes in the future, as there are always new lambs for the slaughter. The

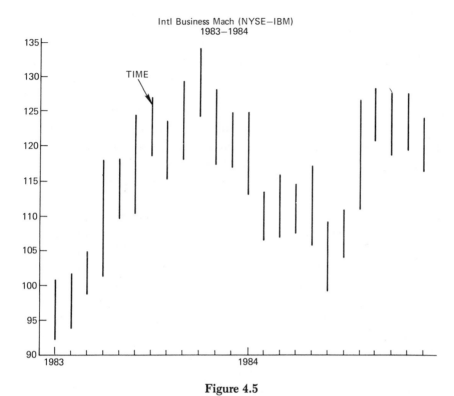

Figure 4.5

PAD investor would be wise to avoid these stocks, and when all others are buying them, it is time to judiciously increase cash reserves. While the absence of a significant number of new issues is a positive sign for the market, the IPO market will dry up long before the general market has hit bottom.

C. THE PSYCHOLOGICAL APPROACH

A number of the technical indicators listed above are really attempts to measure market psychology. Most experienced Wall Streeters will admit that the market is subject to bouts of excessive greed which push stocks to unsustainably high levels, and periods of excessive fear and pessimism which have the opposite effect. (Many academic economists deny that this is an accurate description of the market; their arguments are discussed in Chapter 7.) It is very difficult to observe this fear–greed cycle from the outside and not be caught up in it yourself. Panic spreads in human beings much the same as in animals in the forest, except that modern communications can spread it faster and further. Paroxysms of greed are slightly more subtle, but the famous Dutch tulip craze and later "speculative bubbles" are not that far back in human history.

One valid, albeit difficult, technique to measure market psychology is the much-maligned use of introspection. If you are good at introspection, at analyzing your own emotions, you can feel the onset of fear as the market plummets downward toward a bottom. A certain queasiness spreads throughout your psyche as you begin to doubt your abilities and to second-guess yourself for jumping into the market too soon. Then comes the creeping fear that most of your assets will be lost in the market collapse and the sense of resignation that it may take years to recover to the position you were in a few short months before when all was well. If you are married, you may feel that vague sense of irritation that your spouse will not understand when you explain that the family is getting clobbered in the stock market decline which you did not foresee. In difficult situations like these, which occur too often for my taste, you must constantly fight off the twin demons of fear and pessimism, hold on, and commit cash reserves if you have them. This is the time for patience and discipline. I would recommend reading this section over whenever the demons are on the attack, much as the missionaries read the Bible while in the stew pot. The difference is that if you hold on, you will not get cooked! One key rule we have discussed is: *Do not buy on margin.* This rule gives you extra protection when the market is collapsing toward a bottom: you are not forced to sell.

If you are also adept at analyzing others, you may notice the excesses of fear and greed in your friends, relatives, and acquaintances. Again, you have to resist the temptation to run with the crowd, which is easier said than done. Two ways to make this easier are as follows.

1. Do not discuss the market with Wall Street professionals, including brokers. They are all subject to this herd instinct, being surrounded by the ebb and flow of the market every day. In fact, it is probably wise not to discuss the market with anyone until you have reached the stage where you can do it in a coldly objective manner. This is all much easier if you live far away from the "action," in a small town somewhere in the Midwest or South. Splendid isolation is the best defense.

2. When all else fails, you must keep your sense of humor. You must remind yourself that it is only money, only a game. You should be able to laugh at the cartoon in the *New Yorker* (Figure 4.6) with the caption, "What do you suppose happens when the stock market goes down to zero?" (A special reason to laugh is that *New Yorker* cartoons are a good contrary indicator. This particular cartoon appeared in September, 1974, very close to a major market bottom.)

Some of the most dramatic panic selling takes place when there is a major national or international crisis. When President Kennedy was assassinated in 1963, I ran to the telephone to call my broker to tell him to sell all my stock immediately. Fortunately for me, the market was closed early, just to prevent this kind of irrational selling. The following Monday the market recovered all its losses. Investors who sold Friday were sadder and wiser on Monday.

In the 1950s, whenever Ike was rumored to have had a heart attack, the market would decline too. The Cuban missile crisis of October, 1962 was accompanied by a sharp market collapse, which was followed by the great bull market of the sixties. If it looks like the world is going to end, you might just as well buy stock, because if it does end, it will not make any difference anyway, and if it does not, you have bought cheap and can later sell dear.

The essence of the psychological approach is to gauge the mood of the crowd and then have the intestinal fortitude to move in the opposite direction. You should use any tools for this endeavor that you can fashion. Some on Wall Street refer to the "cocktail party" indicator. When everyone at cocktail parties is discussing or listening to stories of killings made in the market, it is time to sell some stock. If you are not a partygoer, you can still monitor your friends, neighbors, and associates on the job for the same warning signals. Introspection works here too: if you notice yourself bragging about your success or even tacitly patting yourself on the back for your Wall Street wisdom, beware. Those whom the gods would destroy. . . .

"What do you suppose happens when the stock market goes down to zero?"

Figure 4.6   (Drawing by Dana Fradon; © 1974, The New Yorker Magazine, Inc.)

D. SUMMARY

Use a combination of fundamental, technical, and psychological indicators to time your purchases and sales. If the technical jargon appeals to you, go to it with abandon. You can repent at leisure. If you can't abide either the technical approach or the psychological approach, use Rule 1 and Rule 2 to guide your stock timing. These two rules alone, if followed religiously, can protect you from many of the errors of optimism and pessimism of the average investor.

SUMMARY OF RULES FOR THIS CHAPTER

1. The market is OK to buy if Value Line Investment Survey Median Appreciation Potential equals or exceeds 100 percent. Selling should be undertaken when this potential is below 75 percent. 75–95 percent is a neutral area.
2. Do not commence a buying program under Rule 1 if the "Wall Street Week" Technical Market Index has a sell signal in effect.

Readings (and Watching) for the PAD Investor

Encyclopedia of Stock Market Techniques. Published by Chartcraft/Investor's Intelligence, 2 East Avenue, Larchmont, NY 10538. The bible of the elves.

Value Line Investment Survey. Published by Value Line, Inc., 711 Third Avenue, New York, NY 10017. The PAD investor's bible.

Time Magazine. Published by Time, Inc., 10880 Wilshire Boulevard, Los Angeles, CA 90024. Any story about a company or the stock market is worth reading, for the reasons stated in the text.

The *Wall Street Journal.* Published by Dow-Jones and Co., 200 Liberty Street, New York, NY 10281. All the facts are here. The opinions are another story.

"Wall Street Week," With Louis Rukeyser. Friday evening on PBS. The elves have an excellent forecasting record, and, if you don't like Lou's puns, the current level of the index is announced within five minutes of the beginning of the program.

CHARLES MACKAY, *Memoirs of Extraordinary Popular Delusions,* London: Richard Bentley, 1841. Reprinted by the Noonday Press, New York, 1974. Are we any smarter in 1987?

5

THE ECONOMY AND THE STOCK MARKET

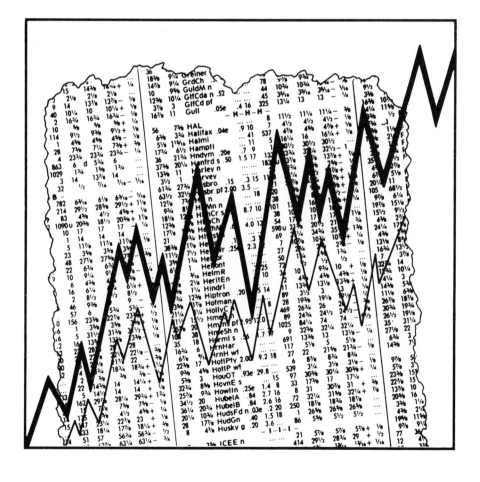

A. INTRODUCTION

Our faith in carefully selected, high-technology stocks, purchased at reasonable prices and held for long-term investment, is in part based on the rosy scenario for the U.S. economy for the next 15 years, which is spelled out in Chapter 6. But it is highly unlikely that the economy will grow steadily between now and the year 2000. We have not learned how to prevent recessions, during which business activity and corporate profits fall. We have eliminated double-digit inflation, but there is no guarantee that it will not return. Double-digit inflation is invariably accompanied by high interest rates, which make bonds, for example, strong competition for stocks, often resulting in low valuations of corporate earnings (falling *p/e* ratios). In addition, rapid inflation is usually brought under control through a wrenching recession, which damages corporate profits directly. All of this unpleasantness suggests the value of understanding a little of how the economy works and what makes business cycles happen. This branch of economics is known as macroeconomics.

A little macroeconomic knowledge can help the PAD investor foresee major trends in the economy that will influence stock prices. This foresight should improve market timing and also help you to avoid being panicked by some of the macroeconomic nonsense which passes for wisdom.

At the end of the chapter, I summarize the basic economic data the PAD investor should watch out for and worry about to protect his or her portfolio. But one chapter can provide only the briefest introduction to the subject. A college introductory textbook, such as the one listed at the end of this chapter, will provide more depth and breadth for the interested reader.

Before proceeding with a most difficult task, I must point out that much of macroeconomics is embroiled in controversy. The views I present are mostly "middle-of-the-road." I do present alternative viewpoints in the appropriate places, however.

B. THE GOVERNMENT BUDGET AND THE DEFICIT

A $200 billion federal budget deficit has achieved the status of the weather: everybody talks about it, and nobody does anything about it. In this section I will explain why we have it and what should be done about it, what probably will be done about it, and what it all means for the stock market.

The U.S. Government regularly pays out (outlays) more than it takes in (revenues). There are three basic reasons why eliminating these deficits is so difficult. First, federal outlays are extremely difficult to cut. Second, taxes, the main source of revenue, are extremely difficult to raise. Third, "tax expenditures" are almost impossible to eliminate. I will discuss each of these points in turn.

Every government spending program has its defenders either in Congress or the White House, and, in general, a relatively small number of beneficiaries of a program have much more to lose individually from a cut than the large number of taxpayers individually gain. An excellent example of this problem is government protection of American farmers. The cost of agricultural support programs has reached $20 billion a year. This is a little less than $100 for every American, but it represents many thousands of dollars to the farmers who share in the largesse. They fight very hard to keep the programs, because their way of life may depend on these payments, but taxpayers as a group do not fight very hard to reduce or eliminate the programs. There are thousands of spending programs like this one, large and small, each with its own powerful constituency mobilized to protect it from the budget-cutting ax. Most may even have made good sense when enacted, but it is well-known that old programs (almost) never die, or even fade away.

Some of the biggest items in the budget affect almost all of us. Spending on social security and medicare is determined by formula, but the formulas are determined more by political pressure than anything else. The recipients of these programs carry much influence in Washington, and it is a fact of life that members of the House of Representatives must run for reelection every two years. The defense budget also seemed uncontrollable until revelations of waste, fraud, and abuse in the Pentagon made it possible to argue for cuts in defense spending without appearing unpatriotic. Still, defense spending will continue to grow, albeit at a much slower rate than originally planned by the Reagan administration.

In sum, we do not have the political will, with or without Gramm-Rudman, to cut expenditures in a meaningful way that will shrink the budget deficit to a less unhealthy level.*

If, in fact, there really is nothing else to cut (which I doubt), we could still close the deficit gap by raising taxes on ourselves. Raising taxes has never been a politically popular action-for elected representatives to take. We resist higher taxes (actually, it seems many successfully resist the current level of taxes) unless there is a compelling case for them. President Reagan's refusal to consider any tax increase in his second term foreclosed a golden opportunity, since the President could convince the public that higher taxes were a necessary evil. If no progress is made cutting the budget deficit, higher taxes may still be a possibility. These taxes would probably be easier to collect if the system were viewed as fair. Tax reform is not likely to make the system much fairer, since again, each "loophole" is defended by the special interests that have benefitted greatly from it. (See Chapter 10 for a discussion of true tax reform and its prospects.)

These "loopholes," which are "legitimate deductions" to their defenders, are called tax expenditures, because they increase the budget deficit by not collecting revenue on income that would otherwise be subject to tax. The effect is the same as a direct government expenditure. As with government spending programs, most were created with the best of intentions. We have used our tax code for "social engineering" for a long

---

*As I note later, not all budget deficits are unhealthy. It should also be noted that government accounting does not distinguish between current expenditures and capital expenditures. A portion of government spending purchases long-lived assets, such as roads, which provide benefits for many years. Yet the costs are all "expensed" when incurred. Although this makes the deficit less frightening, it does not reduce the borrowing needs of the Treasury!

time. But every exemption and deduction, whether for blindness or intangible drilling expenses, reduces someone's taxable income and taxes paid, and makes the budget deficit larger. The Brookings Institution has estimated that tax expenditures for fiscal year 1984 totaled $388 billion. The Reagan revision plan, which is supposed to make the system fairer, proposes eliminating some of these tax expenditures, in order to keep revenues constant while cutting tax rates. Yet every one of the potential changes has been opposed by groups that would lose out if their special tax expenditure were eliminated. Many of these groups are large and include "ordinary" Americans: the deduction for mortgage interest is a good example of a "sacred cow" tax expenditure. Again, the problem is basically political. Without very strong pressure from an aroused public, tax expenditures will continue, and a system perceived as unfair will lead to increased cheating by ordinary Americans. The Commissioner of the Internal Revenue Service has estimated that $90 billion of tax revenue is lost because of illegal tax evasion. This certainly makes the budget deficit significantly worse.

The Reagan administration certainly deserves a good share of the blame for boosting defense spending at a rapid rate while cutting everyone's taxes at the same time, and arguing that the deficits would magically go away. They have not, but we need to assess the actual damage done to the economy today and for the future. In fact, the severe recession of 1981–82 would have been worse without a large budget deficit, because deficit spending tends to stimulate the economy. So the damage of a deficit depends in part on the state of the economy. The damage also depends on the response of the Federal Reserve System. While this is discussed fully in the next section, we can say here that when the economy is not in recession, large deficits can force the monetary authority to either push the economy into recession or allow inflationary pressures to build, and neither is desirable. (Both of these evils have been avoided only with the help of other countries; see Section D.)

Every deficit adds to the accumulated total of deficits, which is our national debt. Many commentators are frightened by the level of the debt, which has reached $2 trillion. While this is indeed a large number, so is the GNP, at $4 trillion. So is private debt, which is larger than government debt. More important, though, is the fact that much of the government debt is held by American households, corporations, and the government itself. Only about 11 percent of the total is held by foreigners. The rest we owe to ourselves. Taxes to pay the interest are mostly returned to ourselves. Thus, the debt itself, to the extent we owe it to ourselves, is not a major problem. Attempts to prevent the debt from ever increasing in the future, through a constitutional requirement that the budget be balanced every year, are a major problem. Aside from the practical impossibility of implementing such an amendment, it would also prevent us from using fiscal policy to stimulate the economy in a recession, or cool it off during inflation. It would also be very difficult to cut a $200 billion deficit to zero in one year. While Gramm-Rudman would stretch the pain over several years, a target of an annually balanced budget at a mandated point in the future is still a wrongheaded way to make fiscal policy.

In summary, the projected budget deficits for the rest of the 1980s and the early 1990s will make it more difficult to achieve economic growth without inflation. We do not seem to have the political will to close the gap, but any action we take in this direction will help the economy in the long run. We will thus attempt to muddle through, and we will, unless a crisis forces dramatic action on the budget. Since the budget deficits forecast for the late 1980s and 1990s may be hazardous to our economic health, they will put a damper on bull markets until they are dealt with in a sensible way.

C. MONEY AND INTEREST RATES

In recent years, Wall Street and Main Street have been both captivated and frightened by interest rates and their gyrations. Not only have interest rates fluctuated more violently than in much of our history, but Americans are affected directly by the changes in interest rates more than ever: in addition to installment credit, whose cost fluctuates with interest rates, many American families have variable-rate mortgages. This financial innovation shifts much of the risk of interest rate volatility onto (unsuspecting?) homeowners. And then there are bonds, which Americans once thought of as much less volatile than stocks. No longer. Most Americans know that Paul Volcker, the Chairman of the Federal Reserve System (the Fed), has some control over interest rates, and that massive Federal budget deficits, discussed in Section B, make matters worse. But to explain it all, we have to step back and lay the foundation. At the end of this section we can answer the questions that demand answers: Will high interest rates choke off economic growth? Will inflation return to double digits? Does M1 really matter? We will also pinpoint important data for the PAD investor to watch. These numbers may foreshadow economic trouble in time for the PAD investor to raise cash reserves before an economic and stock market debacle.

Let's start with the Federal Reserve System. The Fed is generally controlled by the Chairman of the Board of Governors. (President Reagan reappointed Paul Volcker to this position.) The Fed has a number of official duties, but the one that concerns us here is the conduct of monetary policy. Monetary policy involves the regulation of the quantity of money and credit existing in the U.S. economy. The purpose of monetary policy is to promote the growth of the economy without either rapid inflation or severe recession. This is of course a very difficult task, which is further complicated by the fact that the President and Congress also have important effects on the economy through their spending and taxing decisions, which are collectively called fiscal policy.

The Fed may suffer from a dearth of information about what the economy is doing, and this so-called information lag is discussed later, but the Fed is overwhelmed with advice from the Congress, the executive branch, private and university economists, and former journalists. This advice is invariably conflicting, a sure sign that most of it is dealt by players who lack a full deck of economic knowledge. The following sections may add an ace or two to your deck.

How does the Fed conduct monetary policy? The main tool is called open-market operations, which are a little complex to describe, but worth the intellectual effort to comprehend. While the Fed can issue money directly and control the amount of currency in circulation, currency is not the principal way we hold our money balances. Bank deposits, some of which pay interest, and all of which we can write checks against, are the main component of the stock or quantity of money which is in circulation at any time. In fact, currency held by the public and these checkable deposits are what is called M1. We will see that M1 has an important impact on economic growth, inflation, and recession.

When the Fed conducts an open-market operation, it buys (say) government securities, which are not part of M1. But when the Fed pays for what it buys, it credits the bank accounts of the securities dealers it buys from. These extra deposits are money.*

Through a more complex process which I will not describe here, this immediate increase in the money stock can often lead to a much larger increase later. The money stock shrinks in the opposite case, when the

---

*The Fed may also end up buying the securities from commercial banks. The following story is only slightly different in that case. The reader who wishes to pursue the matter further may consult one of the references at the end of this chapter.

Fed decides to sell government securities. Dealers pay for these securities by drawing down their checking accounts, which reduces M1, in general by a multiple of the Fed sale. The Federal Reserve owns many billions of dollars of Treasury securities and buys and sells frequently, mainly to influence the growth of the money supply.

The Fed has a lot of control over the money supply, but not total control. Recall the definition of M1: currency and checkable deposits. When you borrow money from a bank, and it gives you a check or deposits money in your checking account, the level of M1 has increased. The bank has created money in accepting your IOU, which is not money, in return for a deposit, which is money. Thus, the Fed has some control over the amount of lending the banking system can do, but only indirectly, unless direct credit controls are imposed, as in 1980.

Lacking complete control over M1, the Federal Reserve sets target ranges for the growth rate of the money supply that are supposed to be consistent with noninflationary growth of the economy. The Fed then uses the open-market operations described above to try to achieve those targets. (The Fed can also vary reserve requirements and the discount rate, but these policy tools are not nearly as important as open-market operations.) The Fed does not, however, always manage to keep money growing within the target range, much to the consternation of Wall Street. In the summer of 1985, the Federal Reserve once again changed its targets in midyear when it was either unable or unwilling to meet them: M1 growth was exceeding 7 percent, the upper end of the 4–7 percent range set previously. Paul Volcker announced a new target range of 3–8 percent, with a newer base, or starting point, and magically, the growth of M1 was back within the target range. This episode, by no means unique, demonstrates how futile it is to watch weekly money supply figures for evidence of Federal Reserve intentions.

One group of Wall Streeters who watch the numbers religiously as evidence of future trends of the economy are the monetarists. Their intellectual leader is Milton Friedman, a Nobel Prize winner and former economics professor at the University of Chicago. Diehard monetarists argue that the rate of growth of the money supply is the major determinant of economic activity and inflation, and that rapid growth of the money supply must lead to rapid inflation. A slightly unfair simplification of their arguments is that any "extra" money the Fed creates will be spent on goods and services, and if the economy cannot churn out goods and services fast enough, the spending will just drive up prices. Imagine what would happen if everyone in the United States woke up Monday morning and discovered that the amount of money in their bank accounts had miraculously doubled over the weekend. An orgy of spending would probably occur, and as the goods disappeared from retailers' shelves, prices would no doubt start to rise. This is often described as "too much money chasing too few goods." As retailers try to rebuild stocks, factories producing consumer goods will increase their output and perhaps hire more workers, and the process will continue to feed on itself. As more workers are sought, they may be able to bargain for higher wages, which will also fuel the fires of inflation. Once rapid inflation is underway, it is certainly self-reinforcing: if everyone sees prices rising, everyone will try to buy to beat the next round of price increases, and further inflation is guaranteed. Whenever the rate of growth of the money stock exceeds what the monetarists consider to be a rate consistent with price stability, they proclaim that rapid inflation is just around the corner. Milton Friedman himself did just this in a September 1, 1983 Op-Ed article in the *Wall Street Journal*, in which he stated with near certainty that double-digit inflation would return before the end of 1984. He was wrong.

Our money fable can also illustrate the major weakness of the monetarist approach. Suppose that all Americans decided to let the magical extra money in their bank accounts just sit there. No law requires them to spend it. What then happens to the economy? Nothing. Now this nonmonetarist version of the fable is as extreme as the first version, but both make a point.*

In this case, if Americans slow the rate at which they spend and respend the money in circulation (in technical terms, the "velocity" of money falls), an increase in the amount of money in circulation may not have much of an impact on economic activity.

Many nonmonetarists argue that the emphasis on money growth is misplaced, especially since velocity can change suddenly and unpredictably. They argue that the Federal Reserve should pay more attention to interest rates, since they have a direct impact on household and corporate spending decisions and are a better indicator of whether money is easy or tight. Yet it seems that high interest rates no longer can be guaranteed to slow down an overheated economy, nor do falling interest rates invariably stimulate the economy. It takes time, perhaps many months, for the full effects of monetary policy, working either directly through changes in the growth of the money supply or indirectly through interest rates, to be felt by the economy. There are additional delays before the economic data

---

*In the second version, the extra bank balances would probably lead to a fall in interest rates, which should stimulate economic activity. I have ignored these and other details for the sake of simplicity.

are available, too. These lags make the Federal Reserve's task of guiding the economy between the perils of recession and inflation that much more difficult. A partial solution to this dilemma is to give more weight to the actual performance of the economy, that is, inflation and economic growth, since the level of interest rates and the growth rate of the money supply are not really important targets in and of themselves. If the economy is showing signs of returning to double-digit inflation, the Federal Reserve will make money tight enough to prevent this calamity. If the economy is sinking into a deep recession, and double-digit inflation is not a threat, the Fed will follow an easy money policy, with rapid growth of the money supply and falling interest rates, to prevent a catastrophe.

When it does occur, rapid inflation is bad for the stock market, in part because the Fed will use tight money to slow down inflation, and tight money usually leads to a recession and a fall in corporate profits. High interest rates, which usually accompany tight money, also make bonds more attractive relative to stocks. While many readers may already have first-hand knowledge of the effects of tight money, let's use a money fable similar to the previous one to illustrate it. This time the American public wakes up to find that its money balances have been magically cut in half. Many will queue up to borrow, others will put off purchases they may have been planning, and economic activity should decline in the same way that it increased in the first version of the fable. As unemployment rises and goods pile up on retailers' shelves, price increases and wage increases will start to moderate, and the Fed will be on its way to victory over rapid inflation, although there will be, as always, heavy casualties. Almost every episode of tight money is accompanied by a stock market decline, so a PAD investor can profit from "Fed-watching."

It should be clear from this discussion of monetarism and the money supply that the weekly M1 numbers are not the ones to watch. The Fed actually publishes data on M2, which is a broader definition of money, including some Money Market Mutual Fund shares, for example. M3* is even broader than M2. The monthly numbers on M2 and M3 give a better reading of the rate of growth of money, and I think the Federal Reserve pays more attention to them. Of course, the rate of growth of the economy, as measured by the growth of the real Gross National Product (GNP), is of even greater concern to the Fed; and just as important are measures of inflation, not just the Consumer and Producer Price Indexes,

---

*M3 includes large time deposits, term RPs, and other exotica. For precise definitions and historical levels, see the *Economic Report of the President* (Washington, DC: U.S.G.P.O.) February, 1986. Table B–64, p. 327.

but also a much broader index called the GNP Deflator. The GNP Deflator, which is published at the same time as the GNP, measures inflation for all domestically produced goods and services. Wall Street has actually caught on to the importance of these numbers, and stock prices may now be more volatile after a surprise in the GNP numbers than a surprise in the weekly M1 number. All of these figures are reported in leading financial publications.

I also watch indexes of (1) commodity prices, since rising raw materials prices can translate into faster inflation, and (2) hourly compensation data, which can reveal wage inflation, which can also be a precursor of price inflation. These data are also published regularly in the *Wall Street Journal*.

Many nonmonetarist economists and other public policy makers have urged the Federal Reserve to pay more attention to the level of interest rates and less to money supply growth. I have pointed out the fallacy of strict monetarism, but the nonmonetarists must also face up to the fact that rapid money supply growth, if it persists long enough, can create severe inflationary pressure. The Federal Reserve Board of Governors is determined to avoid a return to rapid inflation, and thus they are willing to let interest rates rise and in fact cause a recession, if necessary to prevent rapid inflation. This inflation-fighting resolve could change as the composition of the Board is changed with new appointments. If the Federal Reserve in the future attempted to keep interest rates down and ignore money growth altogether, it could unleash severe inflation. The PAD investor may want to scan the minutes of the Fed meetings when they are published in the *Wall Street Journal*, to discern a weakening of inflation-fighting resolve. A weakening would be hazardous to the long-term health of the economy.

The resolve could be weakened by the arguments of a fringe group of economists and former journalists calling themselves "supply siders." They would argue that my discussion so far misses the essential economic points, except for the fact that tight money can send the economy into a tailspin. The supply siders argue that the focus of both fiscal and monetary policy should be on increasing the supply of goods and services, which will keep inflation down and the economy growing rapidly. All economists agree that this is desirable; the argument is joined over whether supply-side economics, as it is now preached, can actually do it. Most economists argue, quite correctly in my opinion, that there is little evidence that supply-side policies have any scientific support behind them, nor does the evidence of the 1980s change the picture. Two examples should suffice. In spite of tax reduction, particularly for high-income earners, and the creation of tax-deferred IRAs, Americans do not save any more of their income now than they did before supply-side economics was introduced. The promised burst of private saving has not arrived. The personal tax cuts were also supposed to generate so much more tax revenue that the budget deficits would go away. They haven't.

Nonetheless, it is true that policies that stimulate the supply of goods and services or lower business costs can give us growth without inflation. These goals can be achieved by either conscious policy or favorable accidents, such as a drop in energy prices, which ripples through the economy much as the energy price increase did in the 1970s, only in reverse. (The benefits for the American economy of this trend in the 1980s are discussed in Chapter 6.)

In spite of pressure from supply siders, monetarists, Congress, and the executive branch, the Federal Reserve has remained on a middle course that has been called pragmatic monetarism. In short, whenever inflation threatens, money gets tighter, and when the economy weakens sufficiently, money is eased. This middle course is endangered by federal budget deficits of $200 billion per year. If the Federal Reserve does not buy up any of these new securities the Treasury must issue to cover the deficit, interest rates will rise, because the Treasury will compete very hard with private borrowers for whatever lendable funds are available. When interest rates are high enough, they can choke off economic growth, as consumers reduce purchases and firms cut back on expansion plans. If, to keep this from happening, the Fed buys up all of the new government securities, interest rates may not rise for a while, but the ensuing rapid growth of the money supply (remember, Fed purchases of securities increase the money supply) will lead to faster inflation, with all of its negative consequences for the economy. The Federal Reserve thus appears caught between "a rock and a hard place." The clear solution to the dilemma is to remove the pressure created by the budget deficits. We have already discussed how difficult this has been, and it will continue to be difficult with our current spending and taxing system. Although a crisis might bring about action in Washington, foreigners have helped us avoid such a crisis so far by buying up a sizable portion of the Treasury's new securities. This inflow of dollars has kept interest rates lower than they would otherwise be, and thus the economy has continued to grow. (The negative effects of a strong dollar are discussed in Section D.) If foreign investors suddenly refused to buy any more Treasury securities, a crisis would be upon us, and I suspect the Fed would allow interest rates to rise and the economy to sink before it would allow inflation to get out of control again.

We can now answer the questions posed at the beginning of this section. Will high interest rates choke off economic growth? Probably not. The economy grew for several years at a respectable rate with a prime rate in double digits. If, however, the budget deficits are not reduced significantly over the rest of the 1980s, we must depend on foreigners to keep our recovery going. When foreigners stop buying our new debt, interest rates will probably rise enough to choke off economic growth.

Will inflation return to double digits? Probably not. The Federal Reserve's inflation-fighting resolve has not been weakened yet. Significant changes in the makeup of the Board of Governors could change that, however. Does M1 really matter? Not that much. The velocity of M1 seems to change in large and unpredictable ways, in part, I think, because financial deregulation has changed the way we hold and use our money balances. M2 is probably a better measure of money, and if it tends to rise above the top of the Fed's target range, money will probably get tighter, and if it falls below the bottom of the range, money will probably get easier. These tendencies will be reinforced or offset by the current trends in economic growth (real GNP) and inflation.

With some luck, we can achieve new heights of prosperity and well-being over the next decades. If we fail, it will most likely be a result of poorly chosen fiscal and monetary policy. At the end of this chapter, I summarize the crucial information the PAD investor can review to be forewarned of such a policy failure.

D. THE DOLLAR

The dollar has been a sought-after currency in the 1980s. This was quite a switch from the dog days of the 1970s when its value seemed to be in a never-ending decline. Americans feared a weak dollar then, and many fear a strong dollar now. In this section I will explain why the dollar was so strong and how the dollar's value affects our economy and economic policy.

The dollar was strong, or increasing in value relative to other currencies, because foreigners very much wanted to hold dollars and were willing to bid them up in terms of their own currencies to get them. Foreigners used some of these dollars to buy U.S. debt obligations, such as Treasury bills. The yields on U.S. bills, notes, and long-term bonds have been very attractive relative to our inflation rate. This high real return is also coupled with political stability and economic growth. The rate of return is very attractive mainly because the Federal Reserve, to keep inflation under control, is unwilling to buy up all the new debt being issued by the Treasury, as we saw in the previous section.

Unfortunately, the increase in the value of the dollar has had a devastating effect on our balance of trade with other countries. A simple example should make this clear. Suppose an American computer manufacturer is selling computers in France. Suppose also that he is selling them for $10,000, and that the value of the dollar in francs, or the exchange rate, is 8 francs to the dollar. The French selling price is then 80,000 francs (8 times 10,000). A French computer company may be able to sell a similar computer for 90,000 francs, reflecting our technological lead over the French. The American company garners much of the market and makes a tidy profit. Now we allow the value of the dollar to increase, as it has in the 1980s: foreigners buying dollars as an investment drive up its price to 10 francs to the dollar. (This is identical to the statement that the franc has fallen from 12½ cents to 10 cents.) Now, if the American computer manufacturer wants to take home $10,000 for each computer, he must raise his price to 100,000 francs from 80,000. He will then get the same number of dollars when he exchanges his francs. But he will now probably surrender a lot of market share to his French competitor, who can, at the new exchange rate, undersell him by 10,000 francs. If he tries to hold the line at 90,000 francs, his profit margin will shrink and perhaps disappear. This example has been played out in real life by American firms in export markets all over the world. When the value of the dollar rises, either sales are lost or profit margins must shrink. The volume of U.S. exports rises slowly, if at all, and American firms, including PAD firms, lose profits.

The same forces are at work in the United States, leading to a surge in imports of goods from all our major trading partners. Suppose the American computer maker was selling the same computer in the U.S. for $10,000, and the French competitor was charging $11,000 (about the same as 90,000 francs at 8 francs/dollar.) Now when the dollar rises to 10 francs, the French firm can cut its dollar price in the U.S. to $9,000 and still take home 90,000 francs. Score one for the French. Our imports of French and other goods rise, and American firms lose sales and profits at home. Our imports rise far above our exports. Our trade deficit has already exceeded $100 billion in a single year.*

---

*Our "current account" deficit was $107 billion in 1984. See the *Economic Report of the President* (Washington, DC: U.S.G.P.O.) February 1986, Table B–99, p. 366.

Normally, when a country cannot pay its own way in international trade, that is, cannot earn enough foreign currency from exports to pay for its imports, the value of its currency will tend to decline. As in the case of the French, the fall in the value of the franc to 10 cents will stimulate its exports and cut its imports. In a world financial system where currencies are allowed to fluctuate freely, this decline in value, or depreciation, is the inevitable result. Our dollar has been floating freely for a number of years now, but instead of depreciating, it appreciated. The pressure of foreigners demanding dollars as an investment was so strong that it drove up the dollar to levels that severely unbalanced our trade.

The strength of the dollar has had some beneficial effects. The rate of inflation in the U.S. is held down by cheap imports, both directly and through the effects of competitive pricing on domestic producers. The purchases of our debt by foreigners have allowed us the luxury of excessive deficit spending while putting off the "day of reckoning." We cannot be sure, however, that the foreigners will continue to take down as much of our new debt in the future. If the foreigners refuse to buy new debt, then interest rates will rise sharply in the U.S. as the Fed engineers a recession to keep the inflationary impact of the deficits from returning us to double-digit inflation. If the reduction of inflows of foreign capital is gradual, which is more likely, the decline in the value of the dollar should remain gradual, and the U.S. international deficit should slowly shrink. In 1985, the dollar began declining toward a level consistent with a smaller trade imbalance. It was helped along this path by active intervention by central banks. A declining dollar will eventually help improve the price competitiveness of PAD companies with international operations that have suffered with the rising dollar. The increase in our exports relative to imports should also provide a gentle stimulus to economic growth.

The true danger to our long-term economic health is that the Congress and the President may respond to the crisis atmosphere created by the trade deficit and enact protectionist measures, that is, create new barriers to the international flow of goods and services. The damage this would cause, in return for only short-run gains for us at best, is spelled out in detail in Chapter 6. The last time the world traveled too far down the protectionist road, we had a Great Depression.

To sum up the arguments of this section, the dollar will recede further from its 1985 peak and the trade deficit will gradually shrink, with favorable effects on the economy. As foreigners' appetites for our debt securities are slowly sated, the forces which caused a high dollar will continue to weaken. Our debt became especially attractive in the 1980s because, paradoxically, we created so much of it.

E. SUMMARY: WHAT TO WATCH

Fiscal Policy and the Deficit: If the President and Congress can agree to a substantial deficit reduction program, the oversize deficits projected for the rest of the decade, and into the 1990s, can be reduced to a level consistent with noninflationary economic growth and stable or declining interest rates. If the budget deficits are not reduced, they will act as a drag on economic activity, as high real interest rates keep a lid on growth. If the deficits are reduced in a meat-ax fashion à la Gramm-Rudman, we will be attempting to balance the budget whether it is good for the economy or not—a dangerous approach to fiscal policy. If the U.S. adopts a balanced-budget constitutional amendment, the economic consequences will be severe, and a PAD investor will want to invest in Treasury bills rather than stocks, at least until the madness has passed. We also should not expect foreigners to keep buying up our new debt at the same rates in the future.

Monetary Policy and the Fed: The Fed will continue to fight inflation first and nurture economic growth second. As long as inflation is not showing any new signs of life (as indicated by the CPI, PPI, commodity prices, and compensation per hour) and the M2 rate of growth is not well above the Fed target range, money will not be too tight and will not cause a recession. Keep an eye on the composition of the Fed Board, for changes could reduce inflation-fighting resolve.

The Dollar: The dollar should continue to fall, and the trade balance in the late 1980s should improve as a result. Protectionism in response to a strong dollar is the real danger.

Readings for the PAD Investor

EDWIN MANSFIELD, *Economics.* New York: Norton & Co., 1986, 5th Edition. This is a readable text on all branches of economics. I recommend the chapters on money and banking to the interested nonspecialist. All Americans should have some knowledge of economics. The economy is too important to be left to the economists.

LAWRENCE RITTER AND WILLIAM SILBER, *Money*. New York: Basic Books, 1984, 5th Edition. Readable and witty. Parts I–IV add considerable depth to the discussion here.

6

FROM NOW TO 2000

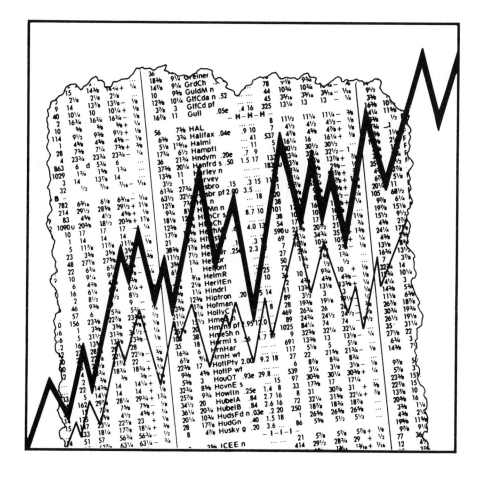

Most Americans are not especially optimistic about the future. There are a number of good reasons why. Aside from the fear of impending doom created by high interest rates and a federal budget deficit out of control, a Third World debt crisis ready to turn into a run on the world's largest banks, and the possibility of expanding war in the Middle East, Central America, and elsewhere, there is the ever-present threat of nuclear war and total annihilation. It is actually quite a trick to avoid a state of continuous depression! Yet most of us manage to do this most of the time. History is on our side. The human race, and the American version in particular, has managed to muddle through somehow.*

In the paragraphs that follow, I discuss the major and minor maladies that have afflicted the U.S. economy over the last decade and make educated and sanguine guesses about their potential effects in the next 15 years. I then describe my view of the electronic revolution and its effects on our economy and everyday lives. I believe that the long-run prospects

---

*Of course there will only be one instance in which we do not. But, if we are going to be wiped out, it doesn't really matter what we do. If you really believe that nuclear war will destroy the earth in the next five years, or even that the Commies will take over, you have been marvelously inconsistent in reading this book, unless you are reading this for amusement in your fallout shelter.

for our economy are bright and that PAD investors will be handsomely rewarded for taking stock in high technology.

A. DEMOGRAPHICS

Demographics is one of the buzzwords of the 1980s. Demography is the study of population, that is, fertility (births), mortality (deaths), population growth, mobility (migration), and labor force participation. Demographics is the application of demographic statistics and projections to business decisions and planning. For example, Gerber Products, which controls 65 percent of the baby food market, must be vitally concerned with fertility in the United States because the rate at which women have children will determine their customer base. Nursing home operators are equally concerned with the number of persons 65 and older, and in particular 85 and older, because these individuals comprise the customer base for their operations. Firms that operate in just one or a few regions of the country and depend on the local population for sales must consider migration trends.

The key demographic element in an economic forecast to the year 2000, however, involves the aging of the U.S. population and, in particular, the graying of the Baby Boom generation. Although the Baby Boom and subsequent Birth Dearth are two of the most significant demographic events of this century, their causes are still not well understood by demographers. Economists, take heart.

The facts are these: the number of births in the U.S. began to climb rapidly after World War II and reached a peak in the early 1960s. There was a steady decline after that, which was not reversed until the mid 1970s. Total annual births in the mid 1980s were about 15 percent above the low point of the 1970s. What this means, then, is that whatever the ages of the baby boomers, they are larger in numbers than the age groups younger and older than they are. This demographic bulge is slowly passing through the American age structure. As the baby boom reached school ages, there was a demand for and unprecedented growth in the number of schools and teachers required to educate these large age groups, or cohorts, as the demographers call them. The college boom in the 1960s was created mainly by the arrival of the baby boomers into the 18–22 year age group. Many colleges and universities found it difficult to expand and then contract physical plants and faculties as the surge of baby boomers was followed by the reduced numbers of the Birth Dearth. Primary and secondary schools faced the same problem.

The next big step for the baby boomers was their entry into the labor force, which was completed by the mid 1980s. The very largest cohorts, born in 1961–1962, have finished college and entered the labor force, and many smaller cohorts are marching behind them. It was not an easy task for the economy to absorb these ever-rising numbers of new and untrained workers. In particular, those not absorbed were added to the unemployment rolls until they found jobs. Even when employed, these new workers had to be trained. Until sufficiently trained and given experience, the flood of new workers was not as productive as older workers. Labor productivity was depressed as a consequence. But the tough times are behind us, demographically, until the baby boomers reach retirement age. This crisis will commence in about the year 2010, and it is unlikely that we will deal with it much before then, since our society is not well known for advance planning on these matters.

Between now and 2010, however, the baby boomers will be aging into the most productive years of their labor force attachment, while the numbers of new and untrained entrants to the labor force will remain relatively low (the Birth Dearth). This will have a beneficial effect on the economy that could equal the detrimental effect of the past swelling of the labor force with baby boomers.

Another source of labor force growth in recent decades has been an unprecedented increase in the female labor force, especially women with preschool-age children. More than half of all married women with children under five are in the labor force now. As recently as 1960 this percentage was 20 percent. Even though these rates may rise a little further in the future (they could drop, also), they reflect a change in American lifestyles which is in large part accomplished. Thus, this source of labor force growth should also be attenuated in the future.

I conclude, then, that the American economy will not be so hard pressed to create new jobs in the future and that the average level of experience of the labor force will rise steadily as baby boomers continue to gain experience. These two trends are very favorable for the outlook for inflation, unemployment, and economic growth. We often attempt to stimulate economic growth in order to reduce unemployment. But faster growth may be accompanied by higher inflation. The Federal Reserve may then slow money growth in order to combat this inflation. If the Federal Reserve tightens too much, the economy sags into a recession with rising unemployment, and we are back to Square 1. Alternatively, if the labor market is not flooded with new entrants, a slower and noninflationary rate of economic growth can reduce unemployment. This was the pleasant experience of 1983–1985.

B. INFLATION AND PRODUCTIVITY

Stagnant or falling labor productivity is one of the proximate causes of inflation. Consider a simple example. Suppose a chipmaker can make chips at the rate of 10 per hour. If the chipmaker is paid $10 an hour, the labor cost per chip is $1 (= $10/10 chips). Now, suppose the chip maker learns how to make 13 chips per hour. If her pay is increased to $13 per hour, a 30 percent increase, will the chip firm's labor costs per unit rise? No. If the chipmaker is 30 percent more productive, she can be paid 30 percent higher wages, without labor costs per unit rising ($13/13 chips = $1). The firm does not then need to raise prices to maintain its operating margin. This is the magic of productivity growth: higher wages and higher income for all without higher prices. On the other hand, with no increase in labor productivity, any increase in wages will cause an increase in unit labor costs. These increases are often passed on in the form of price increases, which fuel inflation. Demographic effects for the next two decades, however, will lead to a more experienced labor force and thus favor more rapid productivity growth. This is very good medicine for the U.S. economy.

The productivity of American workers depends not only on their training and experience (and motivation!), but also on the quantity and quality of the physical capital with which they work. The sheer numbers of tools, machines, and computers are important: more capital means more productive workers. But better capital also means more productive workers. For example, computers are replacing typewriters in the home and at the office. (This book was written with a word processor.) We are all made more productive with this new capital, and as computers become faster and more powerful, we will become more productive still. New technology provides us with this new and better capital, and new technology springs from research and development (R&D). Large investments in R&D by U.S. firms and the government promise us a never-ending flow of "productivity enhancers" which can stimulate economic growth without inflation. Firms in the electronics, computer, and precision instrument industries are at the cutting edge of new technology and should experience rapid growth in the long run.

This growth will not be affected greatly by changing tax incentives for R&D spending or capital spending. Both the R&D tax credit and accelerated depreciation schedules have powerful supporters who will fight hard to keep or restore them, and more importantly, these forms of spending are influenced by many factors besides tax policy.

C. OIL AND ENERGY

The great economic bogeyman of the 1970s and early 1980s was the "energy crisis." It is probably true that in the remainder of this century we will witness a more favorable trend in energy prices for the U.S., which should do as much good for the economy as the energy shocks of the 1973–1980 period did damage. The explosion of energy prices at that time hit the U.S. economy with a double whammy: at the same time that prices of raw materials were rising dramatically, with obvious effects on inflation, the declines in Americans' real incomes pushed the economy into recession. We had the worst of both worlds: inflation and stagnation at the same time, called, for lack of a better term, stagflation. The economics profession was rightly taken to task for having taught a generation of students that these twin evils would not occur simultaneously. But the new lesson has been well learned, and has spawned the so-called "supply-side" movement, which, in spite of rhetorical excesses, helped us to refocus our attention on supply conditions and the long-run growth of the economy.

The rapid rise in the price of energy set in motion several crucial long-run trends in the American economy. First, we have learned how to economize on energy when we produce our GNP. Everything in America is more energy efficient than it was before OPEC. This trend toward higher energy efficiency has yet to run its course, but already we can see the benefits. The amount of energy needed to produce a dollar of our GNP has been falling steadily, with no end in sight. Thus, we can grow without requiring more energy, especially OPEC oil. At the same time, higher energy prices have stimulated the search for new deposits of hydrocarbons, and the reworking of existing fields. The United States, which was supposedly on an irreversible downward trend in oil production, has actually increased production in recent years.* Much bigger increases in produc-

---

*In 1986, U.S. drilling activity dropped enough to lead to a probable reversal of this trend by 1990.

tion have occurred elsewhere, much to the chagrin of OPEC: increased output from Mexico, the North Sea, and other sources have steadily reduced OPEC's share of world output and its influence on prices. Once-mighty OPEC has been repeatedly forced to cut the price of cartel oil, and it is unlikely that this price can be increased sharply in the foreseeable future. Contrary to alarmists' predictions, the supply of natural gas became so plentiful that prices began falling after partial deregulation of this market.

The favorable trend in energy prices in the 1982–1986 period has already paid dividends in the form of noninflationary growth of the economy, and it will continue to do so. Admittedly, the severe recession and high unemployment of 1981–1982 played a major role in reducing inflation and inflationary psychology, but our recovery from the recession was facilitated by falling prices of raw materials.*

The net result of all these favorable trends is that we should be able to achieve more rapid growth in the future, which will translate into higher incomes, rising corporate profits, and a rising stock market.

D. THE RAIN CLOUDS OVERHEAD: U.S. DEFICITS AND LDC† DEBTS

There are two major impediments to the realization of this vision. First, growth in the United States could be derailed by government budget deficits and the high interest rates which accompany them, or by draconian and mistaken measures to solve these problems. Second, the international financial system could be severely damaged by massive defaults on loans to third-world countries. While I discuss these problems in turn, they are related in that many third-world countries have debts tied to the level of world interest rates. If U.S. deficits raise interest rates, the third-world debt crisis is exacerbated.

When the Federal Reserve refuses to monetize the U.S. deficit and does not buy the new U.S. securities issued to cover our revenue shortfall (see Chapter 5), someone else must buy them. The large supply of bonds

---

*This good wind blows some ill. Producers of energy and raw materials lose when prices fall, and this group includes many of the poorest countries in the world, as well as Texas oilmen. The problem is discussed in Section D.

†Less developed countries, also collectively called the "Third World."

depresses their prices, thus raising their yields and interest rates. The deficit that must be financed grew to $200 billion because we cut taxes without cutting spending. Despite Gramm-Rudman, there is little evidence that we have the political will to either raise taxes or cut spending enough to reduce the deficit significantly. Nonetheless, if the Federal Reserve relented and purchased more of the new debt securities, the purchasing power of Americans, as represented by the supply of money in the economy, would grow much faster and would probably lead to more inflation, whether monetarist theories of the economy are right or not. So the Federal Reserve maintains sufficient restraint on monetary growth to keep interest rates high enough to attract buyers for all the new debt securities being issued. The Treasury of course has to compete with corporate borrowers also, for private demands for credit tend to expand as the economy expands. If Treasury borrowing makes it harder for corporations to raise money, some private capital spending may be "crowded out." High interest rates have persisted even though inflation has remained well below the double-digit levels of the Carter years. The prospective real return on a riskless asset like a one-year Treasury note is therefore very attractive, especially to foreign investors. A 7 to 8 percent return minus 3 percent for inflation is a very good return indeed. High interest rates can also keep a lid on stock prices, given that bonds are an alternative asset for investors.

The danger of tight money is that if the Federal Reserve tightens too much, the economy could slip into another recession. This has of course happened before, but it is by no means guaranteed. It is possible, and it has also happened before, that a bout of tight money succeeds in slowing down the economy without causing an actual recession. This is not an easy result to achieve, however, given that no one is sure just when and how tight money actually works on the economy, other than its obvious and almost immediate impact on industries like the housing industry. It is thus crucial for the Federal Reserve to examine the statistics on the growth of the economy, as well as inflation statistics. If the growth rate of the economy remains moderate, with no sign of incipient inflation, the Federal Reserve will not have to tighten credit and can contemplate easing credit. One step that would make this more likely is if the Federal budget deficits projected for the future were significantly reduced by the Congress and the President, through either higher taxes, or spending cuts, or both. I do not, however, advocate reducing the deficit to zero with across-the-board spending cuts and no tax increases, à la Gramm-Rudman. Delicate surgery is best performed with a scalpel, not a meat-ax.

The third-world debt problem is even more complex. It is not true, however, that this crisis must cause a worldwide collapse of the banking system. Many debtor countries will not be able to service their debts fully for many years, and almost all third-world countries will require inflows of new capital if they are to grow rather than stagnate. But the problem is not insoluble. Many of these countries, including two of the biggest debtors, Brazil and Mexico, have implemented austerity programs as prerequisites for additional funding from Western banks and international agencies like the International Monetary Fund (IMF). These programs may enable these countries to stave off default on their existing obligations. It is probably not possible, though, to squeeze the population much more without political crises that would end the careers of those in power in these countries.

Any solution to the crisis must recognize that the Third World and First World (the developed countries) are interdependent. If the Third World is going to achieve rapid gains in its pitifully low living standards, it must import goods and services from the First World far in excess of its ability to pay for them with exports. This excess of imports must be financed by capital flows from the First World. Repudiation of debts will cut off this vital flow of capital and doom most residents of the Third World to even deeper poverty. It may be tempting to repudiate or limit debt service to a fixed fraction of export earnings, in the hope of avoiding austerity. But the piper must be paid: austerity will surely follow a cutoff of foreign credits of all kinds.

But repudiation of debts would also severely damage or destroy many large Western banks, which have made loans to third-world countries far in excess of their ability to repay in a timely fashion. In a number of cases, these loans exceed the total capital of the lending banks. If a write-down of assets made these banks insolvent (i.e., their liabilities would exceed their assets), a banking crisis could ensue that the Federal Reserve would be hard pressed to prevent.

This irreversible interdependence means that third-world governments and Western banks and governments must negotiate payment arrangements on debts that allow the world financial system to avoid a cataclysm. Many countries have already managed to creatively refinance their obligations, which often boils down to a "rolling over" of debts into the future. I believe this process will continue, perhaps in a disguised form, perhaps with a new name yet to be coined. There is no alternative.

As I pointed out in Chapter 5, a strong dollar is still another side effect of high interest rates. Investors in other countries will take advantage of the high inflation-adjusted returns on Treasury securities. To buy them, they must convert their pounds, marks, and yen into dollars, creating demand for dollars on international currency exchange markets. A strong dollar makes our goods and services look more expensive to foreigners, and makes their goods and services look cheaper to Americans. We then import more than we export, and this trade deficit has exceeded $100 billion per year. Normally, we would expect that our currency would depreciate in response to this trade deficit, but the attractiveness of our interest rates seems to have overcome the loss of our international competitiveness. When Americans buy more abroad than they sell, we supply the rest of the world with dollars. But all these dollars are snapped up by foreigners buying our securities, keeping the dollar high. A strong dollar has certainly imposed additional strains on those industries which are already losing the battle with foreign competition, such as the auto, steel, and copper industries, and intensifies their demands for government restrictions on imports. (The dangers of a worldwide slide into protectionism are discussed in Section E.)

The Federal Reserve, in cooperation with other agencies, is responsible for maintaining the health of the banking system. The Continental Bank crisis in 1984 and the Savings and Loan failures in Ohio and Maryland highlighted the fragility of the system. Third-world debt was not the cause of any of these failures, nor does it explain the steady failure rate of farm banks and savings institutions. Mismanagement and bad luck are the chief causes of almost all of these failures. Rapidly changing economic conditions and financial deregulation almost guarantee a continued stream of failures in the future. These failures may tax the FDIC and FSLIC to the limit, but I am cautiously optimistic that the banking system can survive with a little help from its friends, including Uncle Sam. Competition will continue to force out the weakest and most poorly managed firms, as well as those who simply suffer too much bad luck. Failures do not need to undermine confidence in the banking system, as long as depositors still feel that their money is safe. So far, the FDIC and FSLIC have maintained that confidence.

In summary, the Federal Reserve will continue to wrestle with the problems of inflation and economic growth, made more difficult by large federal deficits. A steady fall in the dollar to a level consistent with a smaller trade deficit will be helpful. Chapter 5 contains details of what to watch for in fiscal and monetary policy in the U.S. Stable or falling interest rates and steady economic growth in the West will also help the Third World service its debts without a world financial crisis.

E. A CLOUD ON THE HORIZON: WORLD PROTECTIONISM

Few Americans are aware of a government agency called the International Trade Commission (ITC). Yet this commission now has, and will continue to have, a major impact on long-run growth in the U.S., on productivity, and on inflation. Industries which claim that they have been "injured" by foreign competition can petition the ITC for protection from this competition. In theory, the industry will receive temporary protection in the form of tariffs or quotas or both, during which time the industry will retool, modernize, slim down, or whatever, to prepare it to meet foreign competition to the benefit of all. This is not what usually happens, unfortunately. Protection from competition is a narcotic that is difficult to give up. A recent example was the so-called "voluntary" quota on Japanese automobiles that was originally planned to last for only three years. Not only was it extended for a fourth year, but there was strong pressure for it to be extended for a fifth year, although President Reagan courageously refused to do so. A flood of Japanese imports could still revive calls for new quotas.* I believe that Japanese assembly plants in the U.S. are partly insurance against just such a possibility.

Unfortunately, many other industries also remain protected from the rigors of world competition. It seems the American public is somewhat gullible, or is just misled by the basically foolish arguments in favor of protection. Protection can save jobs only by raising the prices consumers pay for imported and, usually, domestic goods. Economists have calculated that the cost of protection, in terms of extra dollars spent per job saved, is often $50,000 to $100,000. Even worse, protectionism tends to spread through the economy like a cancer. First, each successful attempt to win protection will embolden other industries to seek protection, since it is easier to seek protection than it is to reduce costs and compete. More important than this "copycat" effect, however, is a direct input-cost effect. If American carmakers are forced to buy high-priced American steel, their costs will rise and their cars will be even less competitive versus the Japanese, requiring even more or longer protection. The auto import quotas themselves had a third, more perverse effect: the Japanese maintained total profits by selling midsize and luxury cars with higher profits per unit.

---

*The Japanese have continued to apply quotas to their automobile exports to the U.S., out of a fear of new protectionist measures. A strong yen could, however, ease protectionist pressure.

Since the Japanese are not likely to surrender this market in the future, in the long run American carmakers will lose market share as a result of the quota.

There are valid arguments for protection. Industries vital to national defense, for example, must be supported. Yet it is very difficult to determine just when national security is at stake. For example, must we have a merchant marine to transport troops and supplies in a war? I doubt it, and we have paid dearly for this standby navy.

The spread of protection to more industries in the U.S. will have the short-term effect of increasing employment of workers in the protected industries at the expense of workers in other industries and all consumers, who pay higher prices. If other nations retaliate against us, which is not unlikely the farther we go down this slippery slope, the effects are of course much worse. Our exports will fall, which will reduce incomes and destroy jobs. A general worldwide descent into massive protectionism will sharply reduce the amount of world trade and lower living standards for many of the world's citizens. Ironically, third-world countries may be hurt the most: their export earnings provide the funds to repay their debts to the advanced countries. We cannot in good conscience demand repayment when at the same time we prevent poor countries from earning the dollars to pay us back!

Creeping protectionism can damage the economy in still other ways. First, dynamic industries such as electronics may be driven to seek protection, which will inevitably slow our rate of technological change as the pressures of competition weaken for these firms. A number of semiconductor firms have already sought protection from Japanese electronics imports. Whatever the merits of their case, the industry did overbuild capacity in 1983–1984. But it is certainly easier to point the accusing finger elsewhere. Second, protection will slow the movement of resources out of declining industries and into new dynamic industries, making our growth rate suffer. Admittedly, there are losers in this shift, or protection would not be an issue. Workers in declining industries may be unable to get jobs in expanding industries. I believe these workers should be helped with income supplements, job retraining, and other such programs. But we should not guarantee their jobs in declining industries with escalating levels of protection.

But the world need not return to high trade barriers. Multilateral negotiations to reduce the level of trade barriers have succeeded in the past and can do so again in the future. It is in the best interests of all countries to move toward freer trade. Back at home, the President can veto any suggestion for protection for petitioning industries made by the

ITC, but even better would be rejection of petitions by the ITC. The President can also veto any protectionist measures, such as automobile quotas, passed by Congress. So called "domestic content" legislation is even worse than quotas, and we can only hope that it never becomes law. It takes political courage to confront powerful interest groups like the automobile and steel companies, and the United Auto Workers and United Steel Workers. It remains to be seen whether any American president can consistently do so.

F. ANOTHER CLOUD: THE JAPANESE

Everyone has discovered the Japanese challenge. That probably means it will have little bearing on our future. Just in case I am wrong, I present in the paragraphs below my thumbnail sketch of the Japanese economy and its relationship to the American economy.

Japan's real GNP has grown faster than U.S. GNP for many years now. In fact, Japan has one of the faster growing economies in the world, with her chief rivals located nearby: South Korea and Taiwan.* If it persists, this high growth rate will eventually allow Japan to become the world's largest nation in terms of GNP, surpassing the U.S. Japan will also enjoy a higher standard of living than ours.

I do not fear this outcome, however. Japan's growth does not have to come at our expense. We have grown rapidly since World War II at the same time that the Japanese have grown rapidly. In fact, fast growth of our trading partners and allies is good for the United States, as rising incomes abroad increase the demand for our products and services. Higher incomes abroad also make it possible for our allies to shoulder a larger portion of the common defense burden, which would also benefit us. Low defense spending has certainly helped the Japanese economy grow fast.

Americans who fear the Japanese seem to think that every extra unit of output they produce will put another American worker on the unemployment lines. This fear has of course led to the growing protectionist sentiment in this country that is so dangerous to our long-run growth prospects. The fear really has two components: smokestack and microchip. The smokestack fear is that Japanese competition will eliminate all of our jobs in the steel, auto, and other heavy industries. This fear is of course

---

*Japan's growth rate slowed in the 1970s, in part because of rising energy prices. While Japan may not grow as fast in the future as Taiwan or South Korea, the Japanese growth rate will still probably exceed the U.S. rate.

exaggerated. Consider the minimills producing steel in the U.S. today: they have been profitable (Nucor, Edgcomb, and Worthington are the best examples) at the same time that the largest steel firms have been unprofitable, even with protection. Competition is coming from the Third World, too. The root problem is that our manufacturing facilities and workers are just not productive enough, given the wage levels prevailing. I have seen it written that Japanese steel workers are as productive as American steel workers, and yet are compensated at half the American wage. Wages and benefits in the steel and auto industries are high even by American manufacturing standards, suggesting that greedy workers and inefficient managers have pushed the big smokestack firms toward extinction. This process cannot be reversed, and we cannot blame Japan or anyone else for our problem. By the year 2000, Japanese steel will probably not be able to compete with steel made in third-world countries. I believe the Japanese are already planning an orderly transition out of steel. We could do the same.

The microchip fear is equally misguided and just as dangerous. In short, we fear that the Japanese will overtake us in computer and electronics technology and get all the promised benefits from the electronic revolution. Stoking this fear is the so-called Fifth Generation project in Japan, which is supposed to leapfrog their computer technology far beyond ours by the 1990s.* I don't think that will happen. We are not standing still; our technology sector is pouring out new ideas and new products at an incredible rate. The competition with the Japanese can be a spur to even greater progress in electronics, and our entrepreneurial environment is ideal for this kind of innovation. The worst policies we could undertake would be to stifle this competition, either by government intervention to stop free trade in electronics, or by attempting to pick winners in the technology sector. The Japanese make mistakes trying to do this, and they are much better than we are. We should stick with our strong suit, which is uncontrolled innovation in a competitive environment.

It is unfortunate that the Japanese do not practice the open markets that they preach. Many industries are protected in Japan, partly because there are powerful interest groups which can win protection from more efficient producers abroad. Much of the protection is cleverly concealed under the guise of safety standards, inspections, and the like, non-tariff barriers which foreign goods are unable to pierce. This protection is misguided because it both makes Japanese consumers worse off and in-

---

*The U.S. Defense Department is supporting a Fifth Generation project in the U.S.

vites retaliation by an enraged United States, the latter of which would
be likely to make both countries worse off. The solution is bilateral or
multilateral negotiations and concessions reducing the trade barriers of
all parties. It is our only real hope.

In sum, we need not fear the Japanese. Let us join in this peaceful
competition, in which all countries can win.

G. TECHNOLOGY AND OUR FUTURE

We have driven away most of the economic clouds overhead and on the
horizon. I foresee them providing only occasional rainfall on the otherwise sunny voyage to the year 2000. Technological change will play a key
role in making the voyage sunny. While it is no doubt true that technology
can be used for good or evil—and this most pointedly applies to space
technology and genetic engineering—I have ruled out the cataclysm as
far as investors are concerned. We generally live our lives on the assumption that it will not happen, and I think we will continue to do so.

The electronic revolution will continue to change the way we live
and work, and its effects could easily be as great as the first industrial
revolution. Although we only see through a glass darkly, some of the outlines
of the future are not hard to perceive even now. The basic underlying force
of change is that the costs of computing and transmitting information
are falling continuously. This process should continue at least through the
end of the century. There are a number of applications of ever-greater
computer power available at lower and lower cost that are already evi-
dent; rather than try to make an exhaustive list, I will present a few which,
although relatively mundane, are under way now.

1. Medical Technology

While gene splicing gets all the headlines and may dramatically
change our lives in the future, other changes in medicine have been brought
about by advances in computing and information transfer. The explosion of medical knowledge requires the storage of information and its
retrieval to be done electronically, and there is no conceptual difficulty
with computers being used to do routine diagnostic work on human pa-
tients. While it is certainly true that computerized medicine can be
dehumanizing (and that is a problem with all the technological changes
I will discuss), consider the following possible scenario for the not-too-

distant future. You awake one morning and you notice that you have a runny nose and some red spots on your face. Instead of picking up your telephone to make an appointment with the family doctor, you dial a medical information number that gives you access to a computer diagnostician. You are queried about your symptoms, and the computer can check hundreds of thousands of case histories for comparison with your symptoms and background in an instant. It can order lab tests, inquire about other possible symptoms, and check to see whether "it's been going around." It should also be easy to program the computer to say, "Take two aspirins and call me in the morning." It is usually pretty good advice anyway.

Many other uses of the computer and microelectronics have already changed medicine dramatically. CAT scanners have become commonplace, and magnetic resonance imaging (MRI) and positron emission tomography (PET) may come next to your local hospital. Medical laboratories also require an ever-increasing number of sophisticated instruments and computers in the battle against disease and in the search for a deeper understanding of how the human body works.

2. Meteorology

We are all affected by the weather, probably more than we know, and I doubt that we can change this in a hundred years. I even doubt that we will be able to change the weather, except unintentionally, in the foreseeable future. We can, however, learn to predict it much better than we do now, and improvements in prediction would be of enormous value. Bigger and faster computers are the answer. The earth's weather systems are incredibly complex, and the models that describe these systems push today's largest and fastest computers to their limits. But in ten years, computers will certainly be much faster and larger, and our weather forecasting ability should improve dramatically. The saving in lives and crops will be enormous.

3. Everyday Life

Computers will be everywhere. Our automobiles will be filled with little chips monitoring every aspect of performance, maintenance, and so forth. I for one would dearly love to be reminded it was time to change the oil and filter and check the brakes. These little chips will also store geographic information, so that we can avoid getting lost. For those for whom getting lost is part of the fun of a trip, you can always turn the little things off. All of our appliances will be changed in similar fashion. The furnace will be able to tell you that the thermocouple needs to be replaced. Better yet, perhaps heat-sensing chips will replace this device, which I assume was invented by furnace repair firms. Much of what we write (including books like this one) will be written with the aid of the computer and may be transmitted electronically. Instead of calling Mom when you get home safely, you can send her electronic mail. You may even be able to write a program that will send mail when you are not at home. (Sorry, Moms!) Shopping will become easier if you can find out in advance that the local supermarket is still out of your favorite cereal, and they are much less likely to be out of anything as computers improve inventory controls. Computer voices already announce the prices of the groceries as they pass over the laser scanner.

Computer reproduction of human speech has made much more progress than computer recognition of human speech. Once the stumbling blocks to recognition are overcome, there will be an enormous new burst of applications of computers. Ordinary users will be able to talk to machines without having to master programming languages, software, or other difficult go-betweens.

Many Americans have already experienced the strange thrill of getting money out of a brick wall at midnight. But most of us often still wait in line to cash a check. As the banking industry continues to modernize banking, true electronic banking may become a reality. Current technology is sufficient to computerize all aspects of banking. The biggest difficulty is no doubt the electronic equivalent of bank robbery and fraud. I doubt that computers and the electronic revolution will either create more crime or reduce it. The nature of it will simply change: as we shift more and more toward a white-collar service economy, our economic crime will change in the same fashion.

Our ability to transmit information has improved as rapidly as our ability to process information. Advances in global communications technology have shrunk the world down to McLuhan's global village. In the future, all of us will be as closely tied together as we wish. This phenomenon could make the world a little safer to live in.

All of these changes are quite likely, since they are already under way. Many more changes, which no one can predict, will no doubt take place by the year 2000. It is also quite likely that there will be sufficient demand for all these new products. As their prices fall, the amount demanded will increase. This is of course the first principle of microeconomic theory, but many predictions in the past did not consider just how "elastic," or responsive, demand is to a fall in price. Retailers know this principle very well. A fire sale in which everything-must-go-all-items-drastically-reduced will bring the customers out of the woodwork. Filene's basement in Boston has occasionally been as dangerous to life and limb as the scrimmage line in an NFL game, as customers battle for the best bargains. People can be driven to riot by low prices.

Remember that we are constantly reducing the cost of computation of all kinds. This downward trend may continue indefinitely. The price of a new electronic component that is smaller and faster than its predecessors will invariably fall over its lifetime, which gets shorter and shorter for each new product. What many observers, often including the electronics executives, do not realize is just how much extra demand is created by the falling prices of the components and the falling prices of the machines that use the components. The examples of this mistaken "elasticity pessimism" are far too numerous to catalogue here. A few examples should suffice.

The first complete cycle I am familiar with is the hand-held calculator.* The first hand-held calculator was produced by Hewlett-Packard in the early 1970s and cost several hundred dollars. Even at this price, there was an unexpectedly large demand for it. Steady advances in technology put even more power into the hand-held calculator at a steadily falling price. Few analysts predicted the fall in price or the expansion of the market. Today, hand-held calculators costing $40 have amazing capabilities, but they do not have much of a future. The personal computer, which can easily be made to function as a calculator, will continue to fall in price, while becoming faster and more powerful. In this respect, it is following the same pattern as the hand-held calculator. Every new electronic innovation that reduces computer prices will expand the market. When IBM cuts the price of its PC, the entire computer market expands (although pricing pressures may cut into profit margins of all firms). Yet firms and industry observers still underestimate the market-expanding effects of falling prices. I have two favorite examples of insiders underestimating the elasticity of demand. First, the chief executive of IBM once suggested that the world market for mainframe computers was "about 50." Much more recently, executives of Cray Research, the leading builder of supercomputers, estimated the entire world market for these machines

---

*The anecdotal version of this story can be found in Rochester and Gantz, *The Naked Computer*, p. 24. (See readings section, this chapter.)

at "about 50." Cray itself is now installing about 25 each year, and this number is growing as the price falls and performance is upgraded.

While no one, and certainly not the executives of these firms, can predict where the demand will come from, we can safely guess that it will grow beyond anyone's predictions as the price of computing continues to fall.

Innovations will reduce the time we must spend in household drudgery, such as paying bills or fixing the furnace. This time can then be spent in productive work or more satisfying leisure. Innovations that make us more productive in the workplace give us the same pleasant alternatives. In either case, the standard of living of most Americans rises, and that is good for all of us. Our rising standard of living will make it easier to help those who do not participate in this growth: it is much easier to give the disadvantaged a larger slice of the economic pie when the pie is growing. This idea applies to the peoples of the poor countries of the world also. We can afford to be more generous when our economy is healthy and growing. The wellsprings of this growth are the dynamic sectors of the American economy. PAD investors can invest in tomorrow today.

Readings for the PAD Investor

JACK ROCHESTER AND JOHN GANTZ, *The Naked Computer*. New York: William Morrow, 1983. A fascinating collection of anecdotes and facts about the world of computers. Not that well written or organized, but "bit brains" are famous for their inability to communicate with humans.

RICHARD FEIGENBAUM AND PAMELA McCORDUCK, *The Fifth Generation*. Reading, MA: Addison Wesley, 1983. The first report on the Japanese plan to overtake the U.S. in computers. Another disorganized book—I am not scared one bit, as it were. The whole U.S. is going to be wired with PCs before they get their behemoth off the ground.

HERMAN KAHN, *The Coming Boom*. New York: Simon and Schuster, 1982. If you think I am too optimistic about the future, compare me with the late, great Kahn. He was a worthy counterpoint to the Casey-Ruff-Granville "bad is beautiful" crowd.

EFFICIENT MARKETS?

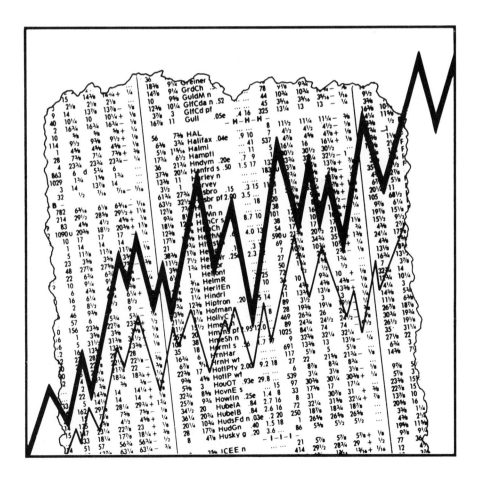

A. INTRODUCTION

Many academic economists do not believe that the advice I am giving in this book is of any real value to investors. I, of course, disagree with them, or I would not have written the book or devised and (successfully) followed the PAD rules myself. Many investors have heard of the theory of "efficient markets," which is the basis for the academic belief that investors cannot beat the market consistently. If this theory is true, investors should ignore all books, systems, and techniques that promise superior performance.

While most Wall Street professionals deny, somewhat self-servingly, that the efficient markets theory (EMT) is true, EMT believers have had an impact on Wall Street. Mutual fund families and money managers have created "index" funds, which are managed passively: the sole objective of these funds is to match the performance of the general market, as measured by a broad market index like the Standard and Poor's 500.* Investors who believe that it is in fact impossible to beat the market con-

---

*Index funds that track the performance of the bond market are growing in popularity also.

sistently can thus invest in an index fund, a diversified portfolio that will always do as well as the market, no better and no worse. Since even the most diehard EMT proponents are willing to admit that there is a very long-term upward drift to stock prices, it makes sense even with efficient markets to buy the market and then hold it indefinitely. (This will certainly reduce commissions!)

Although I reject much of the EMT as a theory based on false assumptions and inadequate testing, I accept some parts of it as essentially true. I therefore believe that it is vitally important for the PAD investor to understand what the EMT is and what its flaws are. This understanding will enable you to both resist succumbing to the "the market can't be beaten" psychology and, on the other hand, to avoid the dangerous attempt to beat the market with short-term trading strategies.

I also provide in this chapter the theoretical basis for belief in the PAD system. The fact that my rules are sensible and that I have profited by them and endorse them is not sufficient. I go on to demonstrate in a nontechnical way how the PAD system is firmly grounded in well-supported theories of human behavior which most economists have ignored. I consider this grounding in theory a much more compelling argument for my system, and it awaits those readers with the patience and discipline to read this chapter.

B. EFFICIENT MARKETS THEORY

The efficient markets theory can actually be "purchased" in three different strengths. In its "weak" form, it can be stated very simply: *it is impossible to predict future stock prices from data on past prices.* If true, this hypothesis is an indictment of all "systems," such as charting, which rely on an analysis of patterns in prices. A head-and-shoulders top, for example, does not increase the probability that the price of the stock will go down. The patterns of stock prices, which are interpreted by chartists, are the result of random changes in stock prices. Even though these random changes often form pretty patterns like "pennants," "islands," and "diamonds," they contain no information which can be used to forecast future changes in prices. This version of the theory is sometimes called the "random walk," that is, the next price change in a stock is as likely to be up as down, regardless of what has happened before. This claim is correctly amended to allow for a very long-term upward drift in prices.

Defenders of charting and other similar systems argue that stock prices do not follow a random walk, but almost all of the evidence that has been gathered shows that they do. (Readers who wish to delve further into this academic literature should consult the readings at the end of the chapter.) Many systems that have been tested rigorously by academics do not make profits large enough to offset signficiant commission costs and are therefore useless. I accept these findings for the most part, with the one possible exception noted in Chapter 3. The major significance of the weak EMT for the PAD investor is that it highlights the near impossibility that short-term and technical stock trading strategies can be pursued profitably by the ordinary investor. (A humorous example of the pitfalls of charting appears in Burton Malkiel's book cited at the end of the chapter.) However, the weak EMT does not imply that investors cannot beat the market; it implies only that *a stock's price history alone will not enable an investor to beat the market.* A wealth of other potentially useful information about a company and its stock is available which could be exploited successfully.

It is also important to realize that the weak EMT (and its stronger sisters) in fact does not rule out the possibility that some investors can achieve above average performance. Thus, the fact that you or I know someone who consistently beats the market does not invalidate the weak EMT. Consider the classic example of a room full of coin flippers. All flip their coins once, and those who flip "tails" must leave the room. All remaining (probably about half of the group) flip again, and again the "tails" leave the room. Eventually only one or a few individuals are left who have flipped an unbroken and perhaps quite long string of "heads." They may actually believe, and so may you, that they have an ability to flip "heads," and indeed the odds of flipping (say) ten "heads" in a row is quite small, about one in 1,000. Yet the result was surely accidental! With repeated testing, it would become clear that a fair coin is going to be flipped heads about half the time, and the champion "heads" flippers will not beat this average by much. If we now substitute stock-picking for coin flipping, and stock winners for "heads," we can fully expect that some individuals and some systems will beat the market by sheer luck. This will happen if the weak EMT is true, and also if the "semistrong" and "strong" variations are true.

The "semistrong" EMT states that stock prices correctly reflect all publicly available information* about a company that could affect the price of its stock. In other words, all that is known about a company that

---

*Those with private, or inside, information could still profit by trading before the inside information became public. This phenomenon is too common to even merit discus-

could affect its stock price is already accounted for in the price. New information, which by definition cannot be predicted, can and will change the price, of course, but the company's balance sheet, earnings prospects, or Value Line ranking, for example, cannot be used to select one stock over another because the information is already reflected in the market price of the stock. In other words, the stock market is "semistrong" efficient. (Since the new information must arrive unpredictably, stock prices will change in a random fashion, thus ensuring that the weak EMT is also true.) The semistrong version of the EMT, if true, would mean that the PAD system, along with all other schemes and advice designed to provide persistently better than average market returns, must fail in the long run, except for successes based on luck. If the semistrong version is false, then the market may have "inefficiencies," or valuation errors, that, when discovered, will lead to above average profits for the finders.

The semistrong version of the EMT is based on two foundation stones: a theory of investor behavior that leads to efficient markets, and a large variety of tests for efficiency using real-world data. I discuss these in turn.

The assumptions that underlie the EMT are not always spelled out by its proponents, but they can be sketched without mathematics, beginning with a few definitions. An *economic actor* is a producer, consumer, or investor who engages in economic activity. Economists ascribe *rationality* to all economic actors, in a very special sense of the term, that is, economic actors know what they want and behave such as to get it, limited only by the means at their disposal. For a consumer, this means purchasing those goods and services which yield the highest satisfaction achievable with a limited budget. For a firm, it means behavior aimed at maximizing profits, given a set of constraints within which the behavior must occur. And for an investor, it means maximizing satisfaction also, presumably through maximizing expected profits, given the willingness to take risks. While economists have developed many unusual variations on these themes, such as the economic theory of fertility and the economic theory of crime, rational maximization behavior by investors is the essential building block of the EMT. Profit-maximizing investors will ferret out any useful information on a company and will, through purchases or sales, drive the company's stock to that level which best represents the company's value at that time.* If somehow the stock price were to rise

---

sion, except to point out that it is illegal. The strong version of the EMT denies even the possibility of insider trading profits, and thus there is no point in discussing it further.

*Information is often costly to acquire, but this does not change the substance of the discussion.

above or fall below this value, these superbly astute investors would instantaneously restore it to its proper value. Now this of course borders on the tautological, in that we are practically saying that the market is efficient because the market is efficient: whatever stock price exists at this moment must be correct, or rational investors would immediately make it correct. This is of course not a falsifiable proposition, which is why most EMT proponents fall back on empirical tests of the theory. Before we turn to these tests, however, I should point out that there are alternative assumptions we can make about investor behavior which are just as reasonable and which lead to very different conclusions about market efficiency.

C. TESTING THE THEORY

Perhaps the most celebrated tests of the semistrong EMT are the performance evaluations of mutual fund managers. It has been repeatedly shown that mutual fund managers, as a group, have not outperformed the stock market averages over long periods of time. Since these managers have access to superb research staffs, pay very low commissions, are well trained in portfolio strategy, and are paid handsome salaries to manage money, one might expect them to be able to outperform the market. The fact that they do not is taken as evidence that the market is efficient, and perhaps it is these very individuals that make it so. Any undervalued stock is quickly discovered and bid up by one or more of these managers to its correct value. If the professionals are unable to beat the market, what hope is there for the (amateur) individual investor? There may be some inefficiencies which the professionals can discover, but, since the "little guy" does not have the resources to find them, they are not exploitable by the small investor. The small investor should then behave as if the market were efficient.

The performance of investment advisors has also been monitored by the academics, again with sobering results in almost all cases. (The one notable exception, the Value Line Investment Survey, is discussed below.) Other studies have shown that new information, when it arrives in the marketplace, is reflected in stock prices in a matter of hours, allowing for no persistent inefficiencies.

The bulk of the evidence suggests that those whom we would expect to beat the market cannot do it consistently, except for the lucky coin-flippers. Even if there are some minor inefficiencies in the market (and there are a few troubling academic findings), these are probably not exploitable inefficiencies for the ordinary investor. For example, certain arbitrageurs may make consistently above average returns with complex strategies involving simultaneous buying and selling of stocks, options, warrants, convertibles, and the like. But these inefficiencies that the professionals exploit are not available to the rest of us. The story is the same for the little-researched company that is overlooked by the professionals. Enormous effort and skill must be employed to root these special situations out, and again the individual investor will not have the time or resources to succeed in finding these pockets of inefficiency. Must we give up, then, and just buy the market and hold? No. Both the underlying theory and the testing of the EMT are seriously flawed. Not only is the stock market semistrong *inefficient*, but the PAD system makes the inefficiencies exploitable by the average investor. I show why in the following paragraphs.

The major weakness in the testing of the semistrong EMT has been pointed out by Lawrence Summers of Harvard University. In nonmathematical terms, Summers' argument is as follows. If we perform an experiment (examine some data) that produces results that are consistent with the EMT, there is a possibility that we will accept the EMT even if in fact it is incorrect. The "power" of a test is its ability to discriminate among competing theories, avoiding this type of error. A commonplace example can clarify the argument: pregnancy tests are not infallible. A positive pregnancy test does not guarantee that a woman is pregnant, nor does a negative pregnancy test guarantee that a woman is not pregnant. The more "powerful" the pregnancy test, the fewer false positives and false negatives will be given. The ultimate in power is a test that is 100 percent reliable. What Summers argues is that the statistical tests of EMT are not very powerful tests and that major inefficiencies could exist in the stock market for long periods of time and not be detected by these tests, just as some pregnant women receive (false) negative pregnancy test results. Summers concludes:

The preceding analysis suggests that certain types of inefficiency in market valuations are not likely to be detected using standard methods. This means the evidence found in many studies that the hypothesis of inefficiency cannot be rejected, should not lead us to conclude that market prices represent rational valuations. Rather, we must face the fact that our tests have relatively little power against certain types of market inefficiency. In particular, the hypothesis that market valuations include large persistent errors is as consistent with the available empirical evidence as is the hypothesis of market efficiency.

This finding casts doubt on many of the studies of stock price fluctuations which purport to show efficiency.

Second, there is the Value Line anomaly. Financial economists have carefully documented the ability of the Value Line ranking system to successfully discriminate among stocks in terms of future performance. This should not be possible, since Value Line is using publicly available information and its rankings and success are widely publicized (in part by Value Line itself). How could Value Line consistently pick winners and losers if the market has already incorporated the information in prices? Clearly, Value Line is exploiting a persistent inefficiency, and the PAD system uses Value Line for just that reason.

The third major weakness in the testing of the EMT is contained in one of the bulwarks of the theory, a scholarly tome written by Clive Granger and Oskar Morgenstern. (See the Readings section at the end of this chapter.) The bulk of their evidence is that the market is efficient, especially with respect to short-term fluctuations, and yet they admit in Chapter 5 of their book that they did find persistent trends in stock prices over periods of several years or more. In other words, the day-to-day or week-to-week movements of prices are unpredictable, but there are longer term trends which should not exist in an efficient market! Granger and Morgenstern claim that these trends go beyond the time horizons of most investors. This rather lame explanation is probably right. Again, this is precisely why the PAD system is a long-term strategy for stock market profits, since above average profits can be made!

These disquieting results may be sufficient to convince the reader that the PAD system can work, since the stock market is not really semistrong efficient. But there is more: the theoretical underpinning of the EMT, the rational, satisfaction- and profit-maximizing investor, is also suspect, undermined by a few pioneering economic theorists who have been publishing their findings in leading journals in the economics profession. I present just three papers from a growing body of work. Two more papers by Nobel-prize-winning economists, which also attack EMT, are listed at the end of the chapter. All of the papers cited refer to still more articles on the subject.

D. NEW RESEARCH

In a 1981 pathbreaking article in the *Journal of Political Economy* (see Readings section), Richard Thaler and H. M. Shefrin (T-S) suggest that rational man is actually subject to conflicting desires. This is of course no news to anyone except economists, and is very old hat to psychologists. T-S posit two selves, called a planner and a doer, which bear a striking resemblance to the ego and the id of Freud. The planner has a long time horizon and must constantly restrain the doer, who wants immediate gratification, that is, "do it, eat it, buy it, now!" The planner knows that this shortsightedness will ruin the organism and takes defensive action to restrain the doer. This self-control, which we are all taught, and a few learn, manifests itself in ways that are inexplicable with conventional maximizing theory. For example, Christmas Clubs were very popular with savers even though they offered no interest. Why? Clearly, this kind of forced saving enables the planner to keep the doer from spending it all now and having nothing left when Christmas arrives. Obviously, the doer has no patience or discipline! T-S present much additional evidence that their model of behavior is supported in the real world. While their planner–doer is still rational in that he or she is maximizing satisfaction given a limited budget and an internal conflict, it is quite instructive to consider the effect that "two-self" investors will have on the stock market. Those investors who are unable to restrain their doers will buy it now, and sell it now, looking for the quick killing, and not exercise patience and discipline. If inefficiencies remain uncorrected for long periods of time, these T-S investors will be unable to reap the gains from waiting. The PAD system is designed to enable you to control your doer with a set of rules and thus profit from waiting.

I believe that most market participants cannot control their doers. Money managers often admit that they are striving for short-term performance, although the real pressure is coming from their clients. Money managers fear, often with justification, that one poor quarter of performance will mean the loss of the managed account to a manager who is "hot." Under this kind of pressure it is much too dangerous to buy and hold stocks for the long term, since they may do poorly in the short term. At the same time there is tremendous pressure to conform to what the other managers are doing. If everyone else is buying stocks in industry X, you cannot afford to be left out if this industry is going to outperform the averages. In fact, institutional buying could be so strong that the industry does for a time outperform the averages. This self-fulfilling prophecy only reinforces the herd mentality. The reverse is also true: when every other manager is dumping stocks in industry Y, you cannot afford to hang on in the hopes that eventually you will be right. The most publicized example of this phenomenon occurs at the end of every quarter of the year, when mutual funds and other institutions (pension funds, bank fund managers, insurance companies) engage in "window dressing," i.e., purchasing stocks that have done well in the current quarter to show them in the portfolio, and selling stocks that have done poorly to keep them out of the portfolio. (There are a number of exceptions to this bleak picture, among them John Neff of the Vanguard Group and John Templeton of the Templeton Group. Both buy undervalued stocks, according to their criteria, and then hold them until they are no longer undervalued. They have been extremely successful for many years, which is further evidence in support of the PAD system approach.) There are more objective measures of the short-term approach of many money managers. A good example is the turnover rate for growth-oriented mutual funds: this figure exceeds 100 percent for many funds, which means that on average their stocks are held for less than a year.

This shortsightedness describes the average investor just as well. One of the great advantages of Las Vegas, the race track, and legal and illegal numbers games is that the payoffs are quick. Sports betting in the United States, a true growth industry, also offers short-term payoffs. This passion for the quick payoff pervades American life, where time is highly valued. Americans in general are loath to postpone consumption compared to many other countries, and even our own in earlier times. Many investors are unwilling to hold stocks for years at a time, and will sell at the first disappointment or the first big rally. For some, the excitement of calling the broker and switching from one horse to another is as important as making profits. I rest my case with one more example. Brokers lobbied Congress very hard to get the long-term gains holding period reduced from twelve months to six. They knew this would probably increase trading volume and hence their profits, since the quick kill gets favorable tax treatment in half the time. It is doubtful that any benefits to the economy have accrued from this change. The doers rule the roost.

Another path-breaking paper was published by Daniel Kahneman and Amos Tversky in *Econometrica*, although a more recent, more readable paper by the same authors appeared in *The American Psychologist*. (See Readings section for both.) In their papers Kahneman and Tversky (K-T) point out that experimental subjects do not behave in accordance with the rational maximization principle of conventional economic theory. K-T find that subjects make systematic and repeated errors in choosing among risky alternatives, which are exactly what investors face in the stock market. These errors exhibit several interesting patterns, but the most significant for our purposes is called "loss aversion." In nontechnical terms, most experimental subjects will accept a gamble with a potentially large loss to avoid a sure but smaller loss, while the same subjects will take a sure gain rather than gamble on a larger one in which there is the possibility of no gain at all. For example, suppose you are given a choice between winning $500 for sure, and a chance to win $1,000 with 50 % probability. If you do not win the $1,000, you get nothing. If you took the gamble many times, you would win $500 on average, winning $1,000 half the time and nothing half the time. Most subjects take the sure $500 rather than gamble on the $1,000. This "risk aversion" has been well documented for many years and poses no problems for economic theory or efficient market theory. The plungers, who are "risk lovers," take the gambles, and the conservative investors, who are risk averters, buy safe stocks. The problem arises in the following experiment. Suppose now that you have a choice between losing a sure $500, or losing $1,000 with 50 % probability. If you do not lose the $1,000, you lose nothing. If you took the gamble many times, you would lose $500 on average, using the same reasoning as before. But if you have already displayed risk aversion, you should take the sure $500 loss rather than risk losing $1,000. But this is not what experimental subjects do! Most who took the sure gain will gamble, or take the risk, to try to avoid the sure loss. The aversion to loss overcomes the aversion to risk. (Technically speaking, loss aversion means that risk-taking behavior is even more pronounced with potential losses than risk-avoiding behavior is with potential gains.) This behavior, which K-T document very carefully in their papers, is quite inconsistent with rational maximizing behavior in risky situations; yet it is quite consistent with observed investor behavior. Rather than take a loss on a stock, the K-T investor holds on valiantly, hoping to "get out even" while arguing "how much lower can it go?" This is a clear example of the loss aversion documented in the laboratory by K-T. At the same time, the K-T investor will point out that "you can't go broke taking a profit" and then sell a stock at a small profit rather than holding on for a really large gain. This risk aversion on the gain side has also been documented by K-T in the same subjects. These behaviors are so common among investors that Wall Street long ago coined the adage, "Cut your losses and let your profits run." K-T investors, if left to their own devices, do just the opposite, cutting their profits and letting their losses run.

The third pathbreaking paper was published in the *American Economic Review* by John Haltiwanger and Michael Waldman (see Readings). This research is the most disquieting of all for EMT believers. All of the arguments against the EMT that I have presented up to this point could still be dismissed by EMT proponents with the following counterargument: granted that some investors are naive, suffering from T-S or K-T disease, for example, and that their decisions about stocks would not give us an efficient market; but there are sophisticated investors in the market who can keep prices "right," and they have the dollars to do it. Haltiwanger and Waldman show, however, that a market with both sophisticated and naive participants can be influenced by the naive ones. By definition, sophisticated participants have correct expectations about the future, while naive participants do not. Haltiwanger and Waldman put these two kinds of players together in two different types of markets. The first kind of market is characterized by "congestion." What this means, in nontechnical terms, is that this market is much like a city's street system at rush hour. The naive drivers will clog up the main arteries as they always do. The sophisticated drivers are the ones who know that this will happen and adjust either their times of departure or their routes in order to reduce their own delays. These efforts by the sophisticated drivers will reduce the level of congestion, and offset to some degree the effects of the naive drivers. (Technically speaking, the sophisticated drivers will have a favorable effect on the outcome or equilibrium disproportionate to their numbers.)

The second type of market is characterized by "synergy." Again, in nontechnical terms, this means that the market is much like the market for personal computers or video cassette players. The more purchases made of one type of machine, the more software or tapes will be available for that machine. For example, as IBM became dominant in personal computers, those makers with machines incompatible with IBM suffered for just this reason. Software writers want big markets for their products, so they tended to write software for the IBM. As Osborne Computer, among others, lost market share, software writers stopped writing new software for Osborne computers, which reinforced the downward spiral toward Chapter 11 bankruptcy. Apple Computer is an exception which proves the rule: continuing sales of the outmoded Apple II family are fostered by an enormous library of available software. Similarly, as Beta lost the battle with VHS for the video recorder market, it became harder to rent movies recorded in the Beta format, which is incompatible with the VHS format. This trend is also self-reinforcing, as new purchasers of VCRs will tend to buy VHS to guarantee the broadest selection of movies, etc.

This synergy in the market means that sophisticated participants, the ones who correctly figure out who will win the market share battle, will *reinforce* rather than offset the behavior of the naive participants. Sophisticated players know that naive participants will display some preference for the less expensive VHS and therefore that VHS will win over Beta. Thus, they all buy VHS to ensure themselves a good supply of rentable movies, compatibility with friends, etc. The result is that the naive participants have a major impact on the outcomes of the battles, since their choices are reinforced by the sophisticated participants.

The best example of synergy is the stock market itself. If you, the sophisticated investor, know what the next fad will be, whether it be uranium, electronics, gold, or takeover candidates, you will buy the appropriate stocks, regardless of reasoned investment considerations, before the thundering herd of naifs discovers them. As prices are driven to outrageous levels, you will sell your shares before the bubble bursts. Similarly, those stock groups which are about to go out of favor with the naive players will be sold by the sophisticated players. Accordingly, prices will be driven down, again with no regard for reasoned investment considerations. (The much-maligned chartists argue that their squiggles on graph paper are supposed to detect exactly this behavior by those with superior knowledge.) The bottom line is that sophisticates reap abnormal profits, naifs lose, and market prices are efficient only for brief moments of time. Thus, successful investors must solve the beauty contest problem of Keynes: pick the faces that others will judge the prettiest.

Admittedly, this demonstration that naive investors can affect stock prices even if sophisticated investors are present has one weakness. Certainly, mutual fund managers must be among the most sophisticated investors. Why, then, doesn't their performance reflect their sophistication? I believe the answer is that mutual fund and other money managers are constrained by clients who demand short-term performance. As mentioned before, if a performance shortfall in any quarter is likely to be immediately followed by the loss of many accounts and thus a substantial reduction in the amount of money under management, it is dangerous to look for undervalued stocks that may not be "discovered" for many months or years. It is much safer to run with the pack. When many managers dump the same stock at the same time, which is not at all rare, the effects on the price are truly dramatic. In the 1970s the victims were known as "air-pocket" stocks, since they fell as fast and as suddenly as a jet that hits an air-pocket.

E. INEFFICIENT MARKETS AND THE PAD SYSTEM

Who, then, is making the above average profits in the inefficient stock market? Not the day-to-day traders, since they are playing against the random walk of the weak EMT. Not the big money managers either, since they are constrained by their clients to play a short-term imitative game. Nor again the T-S two-self investors with weak planners, or the K-T investors either. The answer, of course, is the PAD investors and others like them, who have the patience and discipline to buy stocks cheap and hold them until they are dear, acknowledging inevitable mistakes, but with eyes always on the long term. Even PAD investors can be subject to the whims of the marketplace, but a strong set of rules keeps us under control. If our planners cannot do it, our rules will. This chapter has shown why these rules are so important.

Readings for the PAD Investor

ARROW, KENNETH J. "Risk Perception in Psychology and Economics," *Economic Inquiry*, January 1982. A Nobel prize winner expresses doubts about efficiency.

GRANGER, CLIVE, AND OSKAR MORGENSTERN. *Predictability of Stock Market Prices.* Lexington, MA: D. C. Heath, 1970. A difficult book for the nonspecialist. It makes the case for efficiency, but see Chapter 5.

HALTIWANGER, JOHN, AND MICHAEL WALDMAN. "Rational Expectations and the Limits of Rationality," *American Economic Review*, June 1985. For the specialist only.

KAHNEMAN, DANIEL, AND AMOS TVERSKY. "Prospect Theory: An Analysis of Decision Under Risk," *Econometrica*, March 1979. For the specialist only.

————. "Choices, Values, and Frames," *American Psychologist*, April 1984. Much more readable.

KEANE, SIMON. *Stock Market Efficiency.* Oxford: Philip Allan, 1983. A well-written book for the nonspecialist which makes the case for market efficiency, but also discusses all of the anomalies.

SCHELLING, THOMAS C. *Micromotives and Macrobehavior.* New York: Norton, 1978. Schelling has created models, especially the "dying seminar," which bear a family resemblance to markets with synergy. Quite readable.

MALKIEL, BURTON. *A Random Walk Down Wall Street.* New York: Norton, 1981 (Second Edition). A well-written book by an economist about the stock market, with a humorous send-up of charting.

SUMMERS, LAWRENCE H. "Do We Really Know that Markets Are Efficient?" Cambridge, MA: National Bureau of Economic Research, working paper No. 994. Not for the nonspecialist.

THALER, RICHARD, AND H. M. SHEFRIN. "An Economic Theory of Self-Control," *Journal Of Political Economy*, April 1981. Accessible to the nonspecialist.

TOBIN, JAMES. "On the Efficiency of the Financial System," *Lloyd's Bank Review*, July 1984. Another Nobel prize winner casts doubts on efficiency.

VARIATIONS ON A THEME
Conservative and Aggressive PAD Investing

8

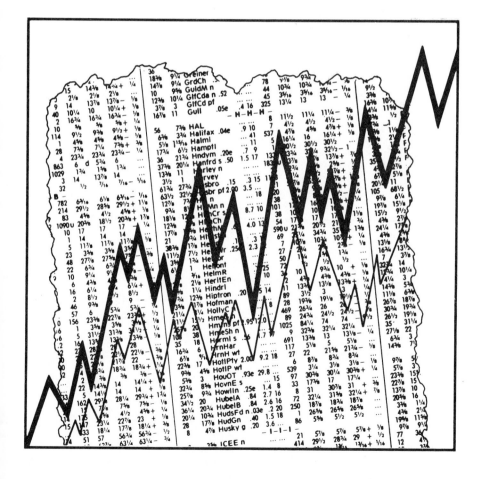

Even if the PAD system seems perfect for you, there are still several good reasons to read at least the first part of this chapter. First, if your existing portfolio contains many non-PAD stocks, it could be costly to liquidate them all at once to create a PAD portfolio. Fortunately, the rules of Section A can be applied to non-PAD stocks so that you can make the transition to a PAD portfolio gradually, as conditions warrant, slowly weeding out fully valued non-PAD stocks and replacing them with PAD stocks from your Buy List. During 1983, for example, it would have been a poor choice to liquidate almost anything to buy PAD stocks, since the technology sector was priced beyond reason. In fact, if this overvaluation were to occur again, during which time the market itself was still reasonably priced, a conservative PAD investor could choose to broaden his or her PAD portfolio with non-PAD stocks, using the selection criteria set out below.

Second, and more important for some PAD investors, my vision of our technological future could be wrong. Perhaps the three industries I have singled out will not grow rapidly for the rest of the century. In any event, even if they do, the ups and downs of PAD stocks are often much greater than the average stock. A conservative investor might not be willing to go along for such a ride, even if the rest of the PAD system could not be faulted. In this case, the modified rules set out below will enable a conservative investor to manage a portfolio drawn from a variety of industries covered by Value Line, including, I hope, the three PAD industries.

Section B is for those experienced investors with nerves of steel who wish to take even larger risks than those entailed in the standard PAD system, in the hope of much larger rewards. The requirement that PAD stocks be selected from the *Value Line Investment Survey* universe of 1,700 companies is restrictive in that it excludes most small and promising high-technology companies traded over the counter. In general, I consider this a virtue of the PAD system, since these OTC high-technology stocks are much more volatile and have a much shorter earnings history and much more uncertain prospects. Yet some of them will grow up into Value Line regulars, and when they appear in Value Line, it will be because they have succeeded in growing much larger, and often their early investors will have already been rewarded handsomely. So a PAD investor might wish to put a portion of his or her funds in these riskier stocks. Patience and discipline is still necessary, and perhaps even more so, given the levels of risk. If you wish to try this aggressive strategy, follow the modified rules of Section B, which can be applied to the small technology companies covered by the *Value Line OTC Special Situations Service* (VLSS). Keep in mind, however, the following cautionary note: although I have in recent years had a portion of my personal portfolio invested in VLSS stocks, using the rules to be set out, I do not yet claim the same personal success for the aggressive variation of the PAD system. *Caveat emptor.*

A. THE CONSERVATIVE APPROACH TO PAD INVESTING

It is not difficult to expand the PAD system to the entire universe of Value Line stocks. While I believe that concentration in technology will have the biggest payoff for the rest of the 20th century, I admit there are attendant risks. The PAD system cannot, however, be applied blindly to non-PAD stocks. In the following paragraphs I review the stock selection rules of Chapter 2 and show how each of them must be modified to admit a more diversified portfolio, without excluding, of course, high technology.

RULE 1: APPRECIATION POTENTIAL MUST BE AT LEAST 100 PERCENT TO THE LOW END OF THE RANGE.

RULE 1C: AVERAGE ANNUAL TOTAL RETURN MUST BE AT LEAST 19 PERCENT TO THE LOW END OF THE RANGE.

While it would be possible to keep Rule 1 intact, it does severely penalize any stock that pays a substantial dividend. I am suspicious of any PAD stock that pays more than a token dividend (see Chapter 2, Section C), but more conservative investors may not want to rule out growing companies that do pay dividends. Even though dividend payments have not been as valuable after tax as capital gains are, they do provide current income and probably some price stability. A moderate-growth dividend payer may then provide a total return (dividends plus capital gains) equal to a fast-growth nondividend payer. Dividends and capital gains are the two factors that determine the annual total return reported by Value Line. These numbers appear just to the right of the 3–5 year price range. (See Figure 2.1.)

I have selected 19 percent as a minimum annual total return to stay as close to the PAD system rules as possible, since an 18.9 percent annual total return for four years (midway between three and five years) will turn $1 to $2, which is the doubling requirement of Rule 1. The one drawback of Rule 1C is that the annual total return numbers do not appear in the Value Line weekly summary index, and thus individual full-page stock reports must be examined to find suitable candidates for satisfaction of the rule and, hence, purchase. If the current price of a stock under consideration is different from the one in the full-page report, which will almost certainly be the case, it will be necessary to recalculate the annual total return based on the current price. A shorthand procedure that will give an approximate annual total return is described in the Appendix to this chapter.

RULE 2: ESTIMATED FUTURE EARNINGS MUST BE AT LEAST 100 PERCENT HIGHER THAN EARNINGS OF THE MOST RECENTLY COMPLETED YEAR (OR THE ESTIMATE FOR THE YEAR IN PROGRESS).

RULE 2C: ESTIMATED FUTURE EARNINGS MUST BE AT LEAST 50 PERCENT HIGHER THAN EARNINGS OF THE BEST YEAR OF THE LAST FIVE YEARS (INCLUDING THE YEAR IN PROGRESS).

Rule 2 needs to be substantially modified if the conservative PAD investor is going to diversify successfully. The 50 percent growth mentioned in Rule 2C is a reasonable compromise which allows for dividend growth to make up for some of the capital gains shortfall, while still limiting appreciation tied solely to a higher price–earnings ratio. In addition, applying the rule to the best year of the last five years should keep cyclical stocks with little growth potential out of the portfolio. In bear markets, I recommend raising this percentage to trim the size of your Buy List. Conservative PAD investors will probably want to rule out companies with abnormally depressed earnings or a loss in any of the reference years.

RULE 3:   A FINANCIAL STRENGTH RATING BELOW "B" OR A SAFETY RATING OF "5" (LOWEST) DISQUALIFIES THE COMPANY.

RULE 3C: A FINANCIAL STRENGTH RATING BELOW "B++" OR A SAFETY RATING BELOW "3" (AVERAGE) DISQUALIFIES THE COMPANY.

The adjustments in Rule 3C may help a conservative PAD investor sleep better at night. All those Value Line stocks that are below average in safety or financial strength are now removed from consideration.

RULE 4:   R&D PERCENTAGE MUST BE AT LEAST 7.5 PERCENT.

RULE 4C: R&D PERCENTAGE MUST BE AT LEAST 2 PERCENT.

A high percentage of sales plowed back into R&D is one of the cornerstones of the PAD selection system. Rather than scrap it altogether, a conservative PAD investor can retain the spirit of the PAD system with Rule 4C. Even companies in mature industries like autos, food, and consumer goods cannot afford to stand still while the world changes. Spending on R&D is evidence that a firm is willing to invest in the future.

Many companies in a variety of industries spend at least 2 percent of revenues on R&D. For some very large firms, this is a sizeable dollar volume. There are in fact a few firms scattered throughout the Value Line universe that spend close to or more than 7.5 percent of sales on R&D. Many are in the drug and chemical industries. Others, however, are in the office equipment, electrical equipment, computer software and services, and telecommunications industries, which will not provide the same degree of conservative diversification, since many of these firms are part of the high-technology sector. Rule 3C should keep out all but the safest of this latter group of stocks. It should not be hard to build a conservative portfolio with an average R&D percentage well above 2 percent.

RULE 5:   SHORT-TERM PERFORMANCE RANKING MUST BE HIGHER THAN "5" (LOWEST).

RULE 5C: SHORT-TERM PERFORMANCE RANKING MUST BE HIGHER THAN "4" (BELOW AVERAGE).

Stocks ranked "4" for short-term performance are risky to buy, but for a PAD investor concentrating on long-term performance, the risk is often worthwhile. (See the discussion of Rule 5 in Chapter 2.) For a conservative investor, it is probably better to play it safe and restrict purchases to stocks ranked 1, 2, or 3.

For a conservative investor, the remainder of Chapter 2 still applies, including the discussions of each rule. And Chapter 3 needs only minor modifications. Thus, immediate reevaluation (Rule 2 of Chapter 3) should be undertaken for a stock that has fallen to a short-term performance ranking of "4," which by Rule 5C is now excluded from consideration for purchase. These short-term "4s" are now prime candidates for a conservative investor's Sell List. Also, since we are using total return rather than just appreciation as a selection criterion, I would build my Sell List with stocks that have a total return to the *high* end of the 3–5 year range of less than 19 percent. This is a perfect analogue of Chapter 3's suggestion for nondividend-paying stocks. My favorite Sell List criterion, however, is still a minimum appreciation potential of zero, that is, a stock that is selling for more than the Value Line minimum projected price several years in the future should go on the Sell List. This criterion is a good one no matter how high the dividend.

Chapter 4 requires no modification. Even conservative stocks fall sharply in bear markets, so it is still important to try to time your purchases and sales in accordance with the guidelines of the chapter.

The conservative rules we have just set out are restated as a group below. Used with the other rules of this book, they should provide superior returns over the long term with less risk than the basic PAD system, although these superior returns will not match the returns from true PAD stocks if my scenario of Chapter 6 is correct. Investors who wish to have the best of both worlds can attempt to blend the basic system with the more conservative one; note that the stock of Digital Equipment, whose Value Line report is reproduced as Figure 2.1, not only met all of the PAD requirements at the time, but also satisfied all of the more conservative requirements.

Summary of Rules for This Section

1C. Average annual total return must be at least 19 percent to the low end of the range.

2C. Estimated future earnings must be at least 50 percent higher than earnings of the best year of the last five years (including the year in progress).

3C. A financial strength rating below "B++" or a safety rating below "3" (average) disqualifies the company.

4C. R&D percentage must be at least 2 percent.

5C. Short-term performance ranking must be higher than "4" (below average).

B. AGGRESSIVE PAD INVESTING: VALUE LINE SPECIAL SITUATIONS

In the previous section, I showed how the PAD system could be applied to a universe of stocks that are less volatile than the high-technology stocks in the electronics, computer, and precision instrument industries. The risks of a more diversified portfolio will be smaller, but the expected gains will of course be smaller too. For those investors who prefer the higher returns that may come with higher risk, it is possible to extend the PAD system to the small and risky high-technology stocks which are covered by the *Value Line OTC Special Situations Service* (VLSS). A carefully selected group of these aggressive growth stocks can well complement a basic PAD portfolio drawn from the VLIS.

1. The *Value Line OTC Special Situations Service* (VLSS)

The VLSS is published by Value Line, Inc., the publishers of the *Value Line Investment Survey*. It is published 24 times a year, on the second and fourth Mondays of each month, and is available in a limited number of public libraries. Each issue contains a detailed report on a newly recommended special situation, regular supervisory reviews of previously recommended special situations, a general news summary for all stocks covered by the service, and a summary index with current advice on all special situations still under review. Once each quarter VLSS issues an updated report on all recommended specials that have been closed out, that is, recommended for sale by subscribers. After close-out, the stocks are not reviewed again.

VLSS has only four categories of advice for each special situation: "especially recommended," "buy/hold," "hold," and "switch," which is the sale and close-out advice. Each new special situation starts out in the "especially recommended" category and eventually ends up in the "switch" category. In the interim, which in many cases spans several years, Value Line's advice can fluctuate between "especially recommended" and "hold" many times. VLSS recommends that subscribers commit new funds to "especially recommended" stocks, although "buy/hold" stocks can also be purchased. "Hold" stocks are to be held with no new commitments made until the ranking improves. VLSS also projects a 3–5 year average price, but does not report a range of future prices that would be comparable to that reported in the VLIS.

A sample quarterly report on a special situation has been reproduced as Figure 8.1. It is instructive to compare this report with the full-page VLIS report of Figure 2.1. Special-situation firms like SVGI have fairly short operating histories compared to companies like DEC, and thus safety, financial strength, short-term performance, and other rankings are not calculated for them. No doubt, almost all of the high-technology special situations would be classified as above average in volatility and below average in safety. Some additional data is available on these companies in their original four-page recommendation reports, which subscribers can obtain from Value Line. If this report is more than two years old, however, it is preferable to write to the company itself for the latest 10-K report. Company addresses appear at the end of the Business section of the quarterly review (Figure 8.1, line A). If the quarterly review is abbreviated, as is sometimes the case, refer back to the original recommendation report for the address.

The difference in format and reporting between the Value Line Investment Survey and the Special Situations Service forces us to modify the basic PAD system rules significantly for the aggressive investor. These modifications are spelled out below.

A —

Business: Silicon Valley Group, Inc. develops, manufactures and markets automated wafer handling and production processing equipment primarily for the semiconductor industry. This equipment improves productivity in the manufacture of silicon wafers and in subsequent wafer processing steps involved in the manufacture of semiconductor devices. Also used in manufacturing thinfilm recording heads for computer disk drives and for processing silicon wafers into solar cells. President and C.E.O.: Gerald M. Starek. Address: 3901 Burton Drive, Santa Clara, California 95054.

Recommendation: Hold

Recent Price: 14¾

Estimated Div'd Yield: **Nil**

1988-90 Potential Value: **112** **(+660%)**

Originally Recommended at **26¾ on May 23, 1983**

Performance Record: **−45%**

Corresponding Dow Jones Change: **+19%**

B

SILICON VALLEY GROUP, INC.(OTC–SVGI)

BASIS FOR [HOLD] RECOMMENDATION

Silicon Valley Group, Inc. is a leading manufacturer of automated wafer handling and processing equipment used in the production of silicon wafers and semiconductor devices. This year has seen one of the worst recessions in the history of the semiconductor industry. Most semiconductor manufacturers have suffered from weak demand for their products and have consequently reported sagging profits and, in many cases, losses. As a result, these companies' need for or ability to purchase new capital equipment, such as that produced by Silicon Valley Group, has steadily diminished. Thus, SVG has experienced sharp declines in shipments, new bookings, and backlog (as of September 30th backlog stood at slightly under $9 million, compared with $20.9 million a year earlier). Despite the reduced margins that have resulted from the dearth of new business and the company's commitment to maintain research and development expenditure levels, SVG remains solidly profitable. The company has taken steps to cut overhead and to scale down production, including a 17% work force reduction in June. Nevertheless, industry conditions seem likely to preclude any growth in SVG's business in 1986. Looking beyond next year, however, we believe that the company's position as a technological leader and its proven ability to make its technology pay off at the bottom line give it outstanding long-term potential, and we continue to recommend retention of its shares.

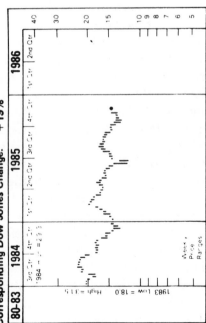

Figure 8.1

1988-90 PROJECTED VALUATION

Sales: **$95 mill.** Shares outstanding: 5,100,000
(18% increase)

Profit Margin: 32 % Projected growth rate: 21%
(1984 to 1988-90)

Earnings per share: **$3.20** Price-earnings multiple: 35.0
Normal Average 3-to 5-Year Price: 112 (+660%)

ANALYSIS

Silicon Valley Group's fourth-quarter sales and earning came in below year-ago levels, as expected. Sales declined 23%, to $7.1 million, reflecting continued weakness in the semiconductor industry. (This figure also represents a 26% sequential decline.) R&D outlays increased to 15.5% of sales vs. 11.0% last year, and marketing, general, and administrative expenses, while lower in absolute dollars, rose to 25.3% of sales from 21.5%. Pretax margins consequently fell to 24.0% from 33.6%, and share earnings dropped 42%, to 21¢. For the full year, sales and earnings were $36.9 million and $1.31 a share, increases of 21% and 5%, respectively.

Although there are signs that the semiconductor industry may have reached bottom, there is no clear indication as to when a recovery might commence or as to how quickly it might progress. As SVG is a capital equipment supplier to the semiconductor industry, its business is likely to lag such a recovery by six to nine months. Thus, the prospects for fiscal 1986 are not positive. We are now estimating sales of $34 million and share earnings of $1.00-$1.05, both of which are below 1985 levels.

W.R.A.

CAPITAL STRUCTURE as of 9/30/84

Debt None   **Pfd Stock** None

Shareholders' Equity $28.5 mill. (4,330,482 shs.)

	1982	1983	1984	1985	1986
Sales ($mill)	12.1	17.0	30.5	36.9	34
Profit Margin ❶	28.4%	33.5%	34.3%	29.4%	25%
Tax Rate	45.0%	46.0%	47.8%	47.0%	46%
Earn'gs per sh	.56	.76	1.25	1.31	1.05
Shs Outst'g (mill)	3.38	4.31	4.33	4.35	4.40
Div'ds per sh	--	--	--	—	Nil
Book Value sh	1.37	5.27	6.56	7.90	8.95
% Earn'd Tot Cap	40%	13%	19%	17%	12%
% Earn'd Net W	41%	13%	19%	17%	12%
Wrk'g Cap ($mill)	4.40	22.0	27.1		
Current Ratio	4.0	9.2	7.3		
Avg Ann'l P/E	--	34.5	19.1	16.2	

QUARTERLY SALES ($ mill.)

Fiscal Year Ends	Dec. 31	Mar. 31	June 30	Sept. 30	Full Fiscal Year
1983	3.77	4.05	4.29	4.84	17.0
1984	5.85	7.15	8.29	9.18	30.5
1985	9.85	10.3	9.66	7.10	36.9
1986					34

QUARTERLY EARNINGS (Per Share)

Fiscal Year Ends	Dec. 31	Mar. 31	June 30	Sept. 30	Full Fiscal Year
1983	.17	.17	.19	.23	.76
1984	.25	.30	.34	.36	1.25
1985	.37	.38	.35	.21	1.31
1986					1.05

❶ Pretax

Figure 8.1 *(continued)*

2. Stock Selection Rules

RULE 1S: A SPECIAL SITUATION MUST BE RATED AT LEAST A "BUY/HOLD."

One of the ways of reducing the risk of special-situation investing is to follow the Value Line advice on new purchases. If the VLSS current opinion on a special is "hold" (Figure 8.1, line B), it is advising against new commitments. Heed this advice. Either appreciation potential is relatively low, or the company's growth rate is temporarily impaired. Of course, it is quite likely that any special-situation stock you purchase will at some time be rated a "hold." I would continue to hold the stock, unless the market rules of Chapter 4 call for a general selling program. Then stocks in the "hold" category are prime candidates for your Sell List. (See the aggressive Sell rules below.)

RULE 2S: A SPECIAL SITUATION MUST HAVE A 3–5 YEAR APPRECIATION POTENTIAL OF AT LEAST 200 PERCENT.

Since special-situation stocks are much riskier than other stocks, potential appreciation must be greater than the 100 percent of Chapter 2 to justify the risks. The rule I use is that the special stock must have 3–5 year appreciation potential of at least 200 percent (Figure 8.1, line C). This rule serves an additional purpose beyond weeding out stocks with subpar potential: almost all of the newly recommended specials have appreciation potentials of 120–180 percent. Thus, a PAD special investor will rarely buy any special-situation stocks when they are first recommended, waiting instead until they have declined below their initial recommendation price. It is usually impossible to buy a special-situation stock at the initial recommendation price anyway, since many VLSS subscribers rush out and buy the stock immediately. This rush forces up the price and drives the appreciation potential even lower. Rule 2S will keep you from "running with the crowd."

RULE 3S: PURCHASE ONE-HALF OF YOUR EVENTUAL INVESTMENT WHEN RULES 1S AND 2S ARE SATISFIED. THEN WAIT AT LEAST THREE MONTHS BEFORE COMPLETING YOUR INVESTMENT.

Value Line itself recommends spreading out purchases of special-situation stocks. This is sage advice. Buy only half of your eventual position when the special stock first qualifies under Rules 1S and 2S. Then wait three months before committing the remainder of your funds. If the stock no longer meets purchase requirements, or if the market timing indicators of Chapter 4 forbid a purchase, continue to wait. Some stocks may "get away" from a PAD special investor with these rules, but that is the price of patience and discipline.

SPECIAL CASE HISTORY: SILICON VALLEY GROUP

SVGI is a good case in point. It rallied sharply to $31½ after initial recommendation. I refused to chase it and waited until it had returned to the $20 level to make my first investment. I added to my position later at $13, and will continue to hold as long as Value Lines rates the stock a "hold." This version of the PAD system is not for the faint-of-heart.

These three rules alone should enable a PAD special investor to build a Buy List of special-situation stocks that are in PAD industries: electronics, computers, and precision instruments. If there is any doubt, the business description of each special situation is summarized in each full-page supervisory review (Figure 8.1, line A). Buy List specials must be bought only when the timing rules of Chapter 4 permit new purchases. Violating these rules will be even more costly with PAD specials, since specials will probably decline even faster than the average PAD stock in a bear market. SVGI is again a good example of this phenomenon. It fell by more than 60 percent in the 1983–1985 high-technology collapse.

RULE 4S: DO NOT PURCHASE ADDITIONAL SHARES MORE THAN ONCE.

The urge to continue averaging down is always strong, and it must be stoutly resisted. Some specials will decline to the neighborhood of zero before Value Line recommends "switch." Do not compound your error by adding to your position more than once.

3. Rules for Selling

PAD rules for selling must also be modified somewhat to account for the differences between ordinary PAD stocks and specials. These modified rules are laid out below.

RULE 5S: SELL ALL OF YOUR HOLDINGS OF A STOCK THAT IS RATED "SWITCH" BY VALUE LINE.

"Switch" advice is similar to a Value Line "5" for short-term performance, but it is more serious, since Value Line coverage will cease and it will become impossible to apply PAD special rules to your holding. Just as important, Value Line does not issue a "switch" recommendation lightly. Trust them.

RULE 6S: SELL ONE-FOURTH TO ONE-HALF OF YOUR HOLDING WHEN THE STOCK HAS TRIPLED IN PRICE.

This rule is a holdover from the basic PAD system and is a crucial one for maintaining patience. Specials often take years to blossom, but when they grow, the growth can be astounding. A number of Value Line specials have eventually appreciated more than 1000 percent.

RULE 7S: SELL ADDITIONAL FRACTIONS OF YOUR HOLDING AT HIGHER MULTIPLES OF YOUR COST.

These trees will not grow to the sky either, and sometimes big trees are felled in the forest. Bank some of those profits!

RULE 8S: SELECT STOCKS RATED "HOLD" WITH LOW APPRECIATION POTENTIAL FOR YOUR SELL LIST.

When the market timing rules of Chapter 4 require you to make up a Sell List and begin selling stock and increasing cash reserves, specials qualifying under Rule 8S should be among your prime candidates, since they are the most vulnerable to a major market decline. Specials rated "hold" but with high appreciation potential are next in line after all Rule 8S stocks have been sold, but these are clearly less desirable sell candidates. I would search my regular PAD portfolio carefully for Sell List stocks before selling these "holds." This portfolio management problem is discussed next.

4. Portfolio Rules

RULE 9S: MAINTAIN YOUR SPECIALS PORTFOLIO AT A MAXIMUM OF 25 PERCENT OF YOUR TOTAL PAD PORTFOLIO.

The risks of PAD special investing are significantly greater than the risks of the basic PAD system. While the potential rewards are also greater, and the discipline of PAD rules 1S–8S should help tilt the odds in your favor, I cannot recommend that a PAD investor place all of his or her investible funds in specials. A bear market could deal a killing blow to a 100 percent special portfolio.

If your specials portfolio outperforms your regular PAD portfolio, this percentage could rise above 25 percent. I would not consider this cause for alarm, but I would arrange my Sell List so that specials are at the top, and if I had new funds to invest, I would not purchase new specials or add to my existing positions.

RULE 10S: DO NOT "CHURN" YOUR SPECIALS PORTFOLIO.

It is tempting to consider switching out of specials that have been downgraded to "hold" and into new or existing specials that are "especially recommended." Resist this temptation. A "hold" means just that. The potential is still there, and specials often require much patience.

RULE 11S: DIVERSIFY YOUR PORTFOLIO.

You can achieve a small reduction in risk by purchasing several specials. I am comfortable with four to six of them. Although these stocks will tend to move together in the short run, eventually the market sorts them out into winners and losers. Do not bet the farm on just one. The lesson of diversification from Chapter 2 applies.

5. Buying and Selling

Follow the advice of Chapter 3. Buy at the market, and sell at the market. The bid–ask spreads for National Market System OTC stocks are fairly small. Remember that we are aiming for tripling or better.

Use your discount broker. Do not make your decisions during trading hours or while on the telephone. Use the rules, make up your mind, and then execute your plan.

6. Staying the Course

Specials investing is bound to exact a greater toll than standard PAD investing, since the price swings are even more violent. Thus, it is only for those PAD investors who have enough patience and discipline to resist the euphoria at the top and the gloom and doom at the bottom. A new PAD investor should start with the basic system first and then, after several years of successful application of the rules through good and bad markets, consider devoting a portion of a PAD portfolio to specials. Given the risks involved, the small PAD investor should stick with the basic system until he or she becomes a big PAD investor ($50,000 and up).

7. PAD Stocks That Are Also Specials

Occasionally a special-situation stock is successful enough over the years to be promoted to review by the Value Line Investment Survey. Analog Devices (see the Appendix to Chapter 2) is just one of several such stocks which have received this dual coverage. If you own such a stock, be governed by the *Value Line Investment Survey* and the standard PAD rules, since the coverage in the VLIS is much more detailed and frequent.

SUMMARY OF RULES FOR THIS SECTION

Stock Selection Rules

1S. A special situation must be rated at least a "buy/hold."

2S. A special situation must have a 3–5 year appreciation potential of at least 200 percent.

3S. Purchase one-half of your eventual investment when Rules 1S and 2S are satisfied. Then wait at least three months before completing your investment.

4S. Do not purchase additional shares more than once.

Selling Rules

5S. Sell all of your holdings of a stock that is rated "switch" by Value Line.

6S. Sell one-fourth to one-half of your holding when the stock has tripled in price.

7S. Sell additional fractions of your holding at higher multiples of your cost.

8S. Select stocks rated "hold" with low appreciation potential for your sell list.

Portfolio Rules

9S. Maintain your specials portfolio at a maximum of 25 percent of your total PAD portfolio.

10S. Do not "churn" your specials portfolio.

11S. Diversify your portfolio.

Readings for the PAD Investor

The Value Line OTC Special Situations Service. Published by Value Line, Inc., 711 Third Avenue, New York, NY 10017. An annual subscription was $350 in 1987. Subscribers to the regular Value Line receive a substantial discount.

APPENDIX: A SHORT-CUT CALCULATION OF TOTAL RETURN

Once you have switched to the total return approach of Section A, it is necessary to calculate the average annual total return on your own. This is not a difficult task, and it can be performed quickly with a $10 pocket calculator. The steps are listed below.

STEP 1: Calculate the yield component of the total return.

The yield component can be approximated by simply averaging the current yield, reported each week by VL, with the future average yield, which appears in the full-page report, several columns below the future average earnings. (See Figure 2.1, line B.)

$$\text{yield component} = (\text{current yield} + \text{future yield})/2 \qquad (1)$$

STEP 2: Calculate the appreciation component of the total return.

First we must calculate the appreciation percent to the low end of the 3–5 year price range. This percentage is just the ratio of the 3–5 year price (low end) divided by the current price:

$$\text{appreciation percent} = 3\text{–}5 \text{ year price (low end)}/\text{current price} \qquad (2a)$$

The equivalent annual percentage can be calculated easily if we assume that these gains occur over a four-year period, since we can then just take the fourth root, or two consecutive square roots, of the appreciation percent:

appreciation component + 1   (2b)

      = square root of square root of appreciation percent

    appreciation component = answer in (2b) − 1   (2c)

STEP 3:   Determine the average annual total return.

Since total return is the sum of the yield component and the appreciation component, simply add the results of Steps 1 and 2.

estimated annual total return =   (3)
yield component + appreciation component

For those investors not of the mathematical persuasion, I offer an example. Suppose stock X has a current yield of 2.6% and an estimated future yield of 2.0%. If we add these two numbers together and divide the total by 2, we get 2.3% for the yield component (Step 1). If the low end of the 3–5 year price range is 20, and the current stock price is 12¼, the appreciation percent is 20/12¼, or 1.63 (Step 2a). The square root of this number is 1.28, and the square root of 1.28 is 1.13 (Step 2b). Subtracting 1 from this number leaves .13, which is 13% (Step 2c). We then add 13% to 2.3% to get 15.3% as the estimated average annual total return based on the current price (Step 3). Stock X would thus not satisfy Rule 1C. Since this is a rough approximation, though, the 19 percent rule for this chapter need not be applied too rigorously. For example, a stock that manages 18.7 percent should probably be allowed to "make the grade." As an exercise, the reader may wish to determine how far stock X would have to fall to satisfy Rule 1C.

OPTIONS, FUTURES, AND INSURANCE FOR THE PAD INVESTOR

9

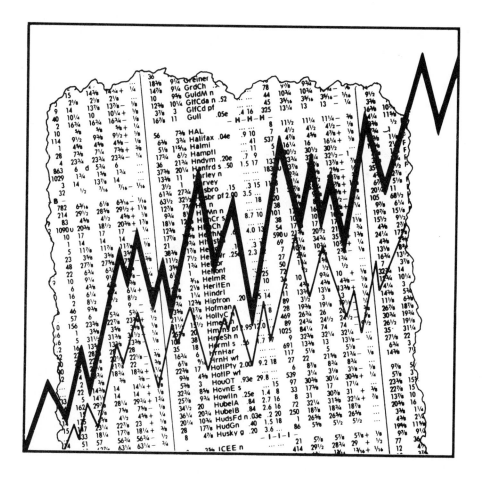

The explosive growth in new financial instruments in the past decade has created new opportunities for the PAD investor, as well as new risks. In this chapter I review some of the actively traded instruments that can improve a PAD investor's performance, mainly by providing some insurance against market declines. The advent of discount commissions has made this insurance relatively cheap.

In the sections that follow, I first review the mechanics of individual stock options (Section A) and financial futures (Section B) and their uses. The next step is to combine the two: future options (Section C) and index options (Section D), which are two variations on the same theme. After mastering this more difficult material, the reader will arrive at Section E, in which I explain why it is important to know about these markets and how to use them in a conservative fashion. I have also included a glossary of technical terms at the end of the chapter.

This chapter may be particularly difficult for the novice investor. However, since the techniques can be applied successfully only to portfolios larger than $25,000, a skimming of the chapter should be sufficient for novice or small PAD investors. When your portfolio has grown past $25,000, and you have earned some investment "stripes," you will be ready

Drawing by M. Stevens;
© 1985 The New Yorker Magazine, Inc.

to give the chapter a more thorough reading. Experienced investors with large portfolios may wish to skip directly to the Appendix to the chapter, in which I present a discussion of a more complex option strategy.

A. STOCK OPTIONS

The oldest form of option is the option on a common stock. The holder of an option has the right to buy or sell a particular stock at a specified price for some time period in the future. There are two kinds of options: *call options* and *put options*. I discuss calls first. Call options give the purchaser of the option the right to buy the stock at a specified price, called the "striking price," until some point in the future, which is known as the expiration date. For example, suppose stock X is selling for $61 a share in June. If there is a market in call options for this stock, there will be someone willing to sell you a call option with a striking price of $60 a share and an expiration date of September for (say) $3. Once you have purchased this option and paid the $3, which is known as the premium, you have the right to buy the stock at $60 at any time until the end of September. If you decide to buy or "call" the stock, it must be sold to you by the writer of the option at the striking price. Obviously, if you just wanted to buy the stock, it would be cheaper to buy it at $61 on the open market rather than pay $60 plus $3 (= $63). The excitement begins when you consider what will happen to the value of the option itself if the stock begins to go up. Suppose stock X suddenly rises to $70 a share in July. If you own the stock, you have made a quick $9 on each share. But what about an option to buy it at $60? The option must be worth at least $10, since the stock is selling for $70! If the option was priced below $10, anyone could make a riskless profit by buying the option at, say, $9, then "exercising" the option, that is, forcing the writer of the option to sell the stock to you for $60, and then selling the stock on the open market for $70. Since your cost is $60 plus the $9 for the option, you make $1 a share in no time at all with no risk. So it should be clear that the option must be worth at least $10, and probably more. If you owned the option instead of the stock, and there was a place you could go to sell the option to someone else after it appreciated from $3 to $10, you could more than triple your money, instead of settling for the stodgy 15 percent gain you would have if you owned the stock and it rose to $70 from $61.

If this is truly your first introduction to options, your hands should be trembling by now. I suggest you sit on them for a minute until I finish the story. Let's see what happens if stock X declines to $55 a share and remains there through the end of September. In that case, the value of the $60 call option will decline slowly and steadily to zero. At the expiration date, it will be worthless, because no one will pay for the right to buy a stock at expiration at $60 when it is selling for $55. The $3 you paid for the option has become $0, which is a 100 percent loss. If you held the stock, you have suffered a minor 10 percent loss, which looks quite good by comparison. The magnified gains and losses are the result of leverage. Your small investment in the premium is tied to the movements of the much higher priced stock. This leverage is of course a double-edged sword, since both gains and losses are magnified. Options have lives shorter than a year, which also appeals to those looking for the "quick killing." Not surprisingly, many unsophisticated investors have been attracted to the options markets on individual stocks. (The put/call indicator of Chapter 4 works well because it measures the sentiment of these investors quite well.)

Now let's go back to the simple example and fill in some missing details. First, who is the mysterious writer of the option you purchased? This individual is often a sophisticated investor or institutional stockholder who is trying to increase the return on his or her stock portfolio in a conservative manner by writing options on stocks in the portfolio. The writer receives that $3 premium you paid for the right to buy at $60. If the stock stays around $60 for a long time, the writer can receive a whole series of $3 premiums from speculators like you who are looking for the fast leveraged profit. It is not hard to earn 15 percent on your money this way in a flat market. If the market falls, the writer of the call option is still $3 better off than otherwise. Only in a rising market does the writer lose out: while receiving the $3 premium, he will be forced to sell you his stock at $60 when the market value is $70. You or someone else will exercise your right to buy the stock, or "call it away."

Call writing is a conservative strategy, because it trades away the potential for a big capital gain for steady income in a flat or declining market. But some writers of call options do not own the underlying stock. These writers write "naked" options that are not "covered" with the underlying stock. Their potential losses are infinite since, if the stock is "called," they must go into the open market and buy it in order to deliver it to the caller. This is clearly a very risky strategy that is not suitable for PAD investors.

The preceding examples have been simplified in a number of ways. First, brokers charge a commission for every options transaction. Discount stock brokers (see Appendix to Chapter 3) also charge reduced rates for options, so commission charges are fairly small, although not nearly as small on a percentage basis as stock commissions. Second, options are generally traded in 100-share units, that is, a single call option quoted at $3 a share gives you the right to buy 100 shares at $60, and you pay $3 for each share in premium, or $300 ($3 times 100). Third, an option that last traded at $3 may have a bid price of $2\frac{7}{8}$ and an ask price of $3\frac{1}{8}$. What this bid–ask spread means is that if you are buying "at the market," you pay the higher price, and if you are selling "at the market," you receive the lower price. The difference usually accrues to the market makers for the option. In general, the more actively traded the option, the narrower the bid–ask spread. This spread reduces the profitability of all options strategies. Fourth, our example used an "in-the-money" option for simplicity. A call option is in-the-money when the underlying stock is selling for more than the striking price. Thus, the option has some immediate or intrinsic value: in the previous example, a $60 call on a $61 stock has an intrinsic value of $1 at that very moment. The other $2 of the premium represents the market valuation of the likelihood that the stock will appreciate before expiration of the option. This part of the premium is called the "time value." Thus, more volatile stocks have higher premiums, everything else being equal, and options with longer lives also have higher premiums. Options with other striking prices will trade at the same time as our $60 call. A $65 or $70 call is "out-of-the-money" since the underlying stock can be purchased for less than the striking price. A $70 call on stock X will probably have a very small premium when the stock is at $61. But there is some chance that the stock will rise over $70 before expiration of the option, and even if it doesn't, it may rise enough to increase the premium on the $70 call, making a profit for the buyer. In our example, however, if a $70 call were purchased and held to expiration, by which time the stock would have risen to $70, the option will still expire worthless! The probability and magnitude of profit thus depend on more than just a rise in the price of the stock: out-of-the-money options are cheaper to buy and offer greater leverage, but are more likely to expire worthless.

Since the creation of the Chicago Board Options Exchange (CBOE), it has been possible for individual investors to trade options on an organized exchange. This has helped spur the tremendous growth of options trading, which is now carried on by the other stock exchanges, including the NYSE, the AMEX, and the regional exchanges, as well as the CBOE, which is still the largest options exchange. In 1985, options trading expanded to OTC stocks traded on the NASDAQ system. Although listed options have been subject to abuses by floor traders and large investors (often at the expense of the ordinary investor), they are still a vast improvement over the old options trading system, which had no resale market and a much smaller set of choices of options.

The mirror image of the call option is known as a put option. When you purchase a put option from the writer, you have purchased the right to sell a stock at a specified price, the striking price, until the expiration date of the option. Using the same example as before, you might buy a put option for $3 on stock X, with a striking price of $60, with the stock trading at $61. (This is an out-of-the-money option, since it has no immediate realizable, or intrinsic, value.) If you own the stock, and it declines to $55 before the expiration date (September again), the value of the put option will increase to at least $5. Using the same logic as in the call option example, if you can sell a stock to someone at $60 when you can buy it at the same time at $55 in the open market, you would make a riskless profit of $5 a share. Anyone would pay up to $5 for the privilege of doing this, so the option, which gives you this privilege, will sell for at least $5. Now, if you own the stock, the decline in the stock price will be offset to some degree by the increase in the value of the put option. This is a form of insurance, which pays off when the market declines. Of course, this insurance is not free, either. The premium on the put option is just like an insurance premium: you pay it in advance and do not get it back. In a rising market, stock X may rise to $70 a share, but you have not made the full $10-a-share profit, since you bought put option insurance for $3 a share. This state of affairs is still preferable to the bear market alternative, much as paying fire insurance premiums is normally preferable to collecting on your policy after your house has burned down.

Buyers of put options do not have to own the underlying stock either. Buying "naked" puts is extremely profitable when the market declines. In the example above, the put buyer would see the value of his option on stock X rise from $3 to over $5, which is a large percentage gain, much more than could be achieved by selling short on 50 percent margin. (As noted in Chapter 4, when stocks are falling, unsophisticated investors begin to buy put options in large numbers, and a sharp rise in the put/call ratio usually signals a market bottom.)

The writers of put options are sometimes conservative investors. You can "lock in" a price for a stock you want to buy by writing a put option. If the price rises, the put option will become worthless, and the option writer keeps the premium. Using our example again, when stock X is selling for $70 and the September $60 put option is about to expire, who will pay for the right to sell the stock to someone at $60 when the stock can be sold in the open market for $70? No one will, and the option expires worthless. If the stock declines to $55, the writer of the option may get the stock "put," or sold, to him. Remember that a put option gives the buyer the right to sell the stock to the writer for $60. You may want to do this when the market price is $55, since the writer must then pay you $60. His net cost is, however, lower, since he received a $3 premium from you at the outset. When the stock was $61, the writer "locked in" a price of $57 a share ($60 − $3 premium). Many put writers have no desire to have the stock put to them. They are simply hoping to pocket the premium. Other put writers may be employing complex strategies involving multiple stock and options positions.

The organized markets for options on individual stocks have grown in size almost continuously for a decade. Most actively traded stocks (including most PAD stocks) have options traded on them. In addition, at any point in time, there are different call and put options being traded for the same stock. Thus, for stock X, there may be simultaneous trading in call options expiring in September with striking prices of $50, $55, $60, and $65, and additional sets of options may be trading with expiration dates in December and March. An entire set of put options may be trading too. An example of part of the *Wall Street Journal's* daily report on options trading appears as Figure 9.1. (It includes the all-important summary for the CBOE of put and call volume.) Looking at the figure, we can see that ITT Corp., for example, closed at $35 a share on October 14, 1985. The December $35 call option, which was "at-the-money," finished the day at 2⅜. The December $30 call option, which was in-the-money, closed at 5½, while the $40 option for the same month sold for 15/16. The December $35 put option finished the day at $2, with the December $30 put (out-of-the-money) much cheaper, and the $40 put, which was in-the-money, much more expensive. Options were also trading with expirations in March and June, although entries of "r" mean that there was no trading in several of the options. (It is interesting to note that the market placed a slightly higher value on the $35 call than the $35 put; this is in part a sign of the

LISTED OPTIONS QUOTATIONS

Monday, October 14, 1985

Closing prices of all options. Sales unit usually is 100 shares.
Stock close is New York or American exchange final price.

Option & NY Close	Strike Price	Calls—Last			Puts—Last		
		Nov	Feb	May	Nov	Feb	May
21	... 22½	r	¼	r	r	r	r
21	 25	r	1-16	r	r	r	r
Am Hos	35	12¾	r	s	r	r	s
47½	... 40	8⅛	8¼	r	⅜	1	r
47½	... 45	3¾	4¾	r	1	1 13-16	r
47½	... 50	3-16	⅞	r	2⅞	r	r
AlnGrp	.. 70	20¾	s	s	r	s	s
90½	... 75	16¼	s	s	r	s	s
90½	... 80	11½	12½	r	⅛	1	r
90½	... 85	6¾	8½	r	½	r	r
90½	... 90	2⅝	4¼	6¼	1¾	r	r
90½	... 95	⅝	2¼	s	r	r	s
Amoco o	.65	4¼	r	s	r	r	s
Amoco	.. 65	3¼	4⅛	5	½	1⅝	2½
67¾	... 70	9-16	1⅝	r	r	3½	r
A M P	.. 25	r	r	r	⅛	r	r
29⅝	... 30	⅞	2	2¾	1 3-16	2¼	3
29⅝	... 35	r	r	r	r	5¾	6
Baxter	12½	1⅜	1⅝	2⅛	3-16	r	r
13¾	... 15	⅛	7-16	¾	1½	1¾	r
13¾	. 17½	1-16	3-16	s	r	r	s
Blk Dk	17½	r	1⅝	r	r	r	r
18¼	... 20	r	9-16	⅞	1⅞	r	2
Boeing	.. 40	4⅞	5⅜	r	⅜	1	r
44⅜	... 45	1⅜	3⅛	4¼	1⅞	3⅛	3¾
44⅜	... 50	¼	1¼	2	6⅛	r	r
44⅜	... 55	1-16	½	s	r	r	s
Boeing o	.40	r	5⅞	s	r	r	s
44⅜	. 46⅝	11-16	r	s	r	r	s
Bois C	...35	r	7	s	r	r	s
42¼	... 40	r	4	r	r	1½	2
42¼	... 45	½	r	r	3	r	r
[illegible]	50	⅛	⅝	1⅛	r	r	r

Option & NY Close	Strike Price	Calls—Last			Puts—Last		
		Dec	Mar	Jun	Dec	Mar	Jun
HughTI	..10	2½	r	r	1-16	r	r
12⅜	. 12½	½	15-16	r	r	11-16	r
12⅜	... 15	1-16	r	7-16	2⅜	r	r
I T T	30	5½	6¼	r	3-16	½	r
35	 35	2⅜	3¼	3⅝	2	2½	2¾
35	 40	15-16	1⅝	2	5⅜	5½	r
K mart	..30	2⅞	3¼	3¾	7-16	r	r
32⅜	... 35	7-16	15-16	1 7-16	3½	3½	r
32⅜	... 40	1-16	¼	s	r	r	s
Litton	... 65	7¼	r	r	½	1½	r
70¼	... 70	3¾	5½	r	r	3½	r
70¼	... 75	1¼	r	r	r	6	r
70¼	... 80	r	r	r	9⅛	9¾	r
70¼	... 85	3-16	r	r	r	r	r
Loews	.. 40	r	6⅜	r	r	r	r
45⅛	... 50	⅜	1¼	2⅛	r	r	r
MaryK	.. 10	3⅜	r	r	⅛	r	r
13¼	. 12½	1½	1¾	r	½	r	r
13¼	... 15	1-16	r	r	r	r	r
Mc Don	. 55	r	s	s	1-16	s	s
66⅛	... 60	r	r	r	5-16	¾	r
66⅛	... 65	2⅝	4¼	r	1⅛	r	r
66⅛	... 70	¾	2	r	r	r	r
66⅛	... 75	3-16	⅝	s	r	r	s
Mid SU	.7½	r	2⅜	2 13-16	1-16	¼	5-16
9½	 10	⅜	13-16	1 1-16	¾	1	1⅛
9½	.. 12½	1-16	3-16	s	3⅛	3⅛	s
9½	 15	r	1-16	s	r	r	s
N C R	...25	8½	r	s	r	r	s
34¼	... 30	4½	4¾	r	⅜	1	r
34¼	... 35	1¼	2 1-16	2¼	1⅝	2½	r
34¼	... 40	3-16	½	s	r	r	s
NorSo	... 65	r	4⅝	r	r	r	r

Figure 9.1

(Reprinted by permission of the *Wall Street Journal* © Dow Jones & Company Inc., 1985.

basic bullishness of the average option buyer.) For those investors who wish to study options trading in more detail, there are several books and booklets cited at the end of this chapter which are good introductions to the subject. They all explain a variety of complex multioption strategies, and the books contain valuation models for option pricing. Our purpose in presenting just a bare-bones description of the option market is to set the stage for discussion of stock index futures options and stock index options, which can be used by the PAD investor as portfolio insurance. Before we can do this, however, we must explain how futures markets work.

B. STOCK INDEX FUTURES

Until 1982, it was impossible for the ordinary investor to "buy the market." For those investors who were more adept at guessing overall market trends than they were at picking individual stocks, and especially those investors and speculators who knew that the market just had to go up or down that day, there was no direct and simple way to bet on their convictions. In 1982, stock index futures trading began, and these investors and others could bet on the market every day until their stakes ran out.

The largest market for stock index futures trading is housed at the Chicago Mercantile Exchange (CME), which was once better known as the home of frozen pork belly trading. The CME futures contract is based on the Standard and Poor's 500 Index, a well-known market barometer composed of the stocks of 500 large companies. Trading rules are quite similar to those for frozen pork bellies: a buyer of a futures contract agrees to purchase the underlying commodity for a specific price at the expiration of trading of the contract. For example, you could buy a futures contract for frozen pork bellies to be delivered to you in July for, say, 65 cents a pound. You could buy the contract in October of the previous year, and if you are a bacon merchant, you have fixed your raw materials costs for next July well in advance. If you are in the slaughtering business, you could be the seller of this contract and lock in a price for your product in advance. If you kept large quantities of pork bellies in storage, you could also use the futures market to hedge, that is, protect yourself, against losses in the value of your inventory. In this case, you are not interested in taking or making delivery of the pork. But if you do agree to deliver bellies at 65 cents a pound next July, and in the interim the cash price of pork bellies declines, the price of the July futures contract will also probably decline, and the decline in the value of your inventory could be offset in full or in part by the decline in the futures market. Thus, if pork bellies for July delivery fall to 62 cents a pound, you can buy back the contract you sold at 65 cents and make a three-cent-a-pound profit. (The only unusual feature of this transaction is that you have sold before you bought.) If the value of your inventory has fallen by three cents a pound, your inventory loss can be fully offset by your futures gain. Of course, if futures prices and cash prices rise, the loss on the futures contract can offset the gain on your inventory.

This reduction of uncertainty for buyers, sellers, and inventory holders has economic value for all concerned, and thus futures markets have persisted in the face of flagrant trading abuses and criticism from many quarters, including some farmers, who are convinced that low farm prices are the fault of the futures exchanges.

But anyone can buy or sell a futures contract. If you think that the price of pork bellies is going to rise, you can buy a pork belly contract through a commodities broker. Since the product will not be exchanged until next July, the broker only requires you to put up a good faith deposit, to protect the broker if pork bellies decline instead of rise. The margin deposit is only a fraction of the value of the contract, so leverage again magnifies the result and attracts the little speculators to their doom. Every change in the value of the contract is charged against, or added to, your margin deposit. One pork belly contract covers 40,000 pounds and at 65 cents per pound is worth almost $25,000. The margin deposit is often as low as $2,500. Thus, if the value of the contract declines 10 percent, from $25,000 to $22,500, your entire margin deposit will be lost. The broker will sell your contract before this happens, in order to protect the brokerage firm from additional losses that you cannot make up. If you send the broker more money, you can continue to hold a losing position, although almost all commodity traders advise against "meeting a margin call." Now it could also happen that the pork belly price rises by 10 percent, and the contract is now worth $27,500. In this case, you keep all of the $2,500 gain in value as your profit, doubling your money.

The sad truth is that most public commodity speculators lose money, just as most little porkers end up in the supermarket case. The futures pits are no place for a PAD investor. (For further proof, see Chapter 10.) Yet, the futures industry has created financial futures that can provide conservative opportunities for the PAD investor. It is to these new instruments that we now turn.

Futures on the Standard and Poor's 500 index are actively traded on the CME, with daily volume often larger than all of the traditional

CME markets combined. The only major difference between S&P 500 futures and pork bellies is that the underlying commodity, the S&P 500, cannot be delivered against the futures contract at the expiration date. All contracts are "settled" in cash, for those holding contracts at the expiration date, based on the final S&P 500 index at the end of trading. In this sense, buyers and sellers of the futures are simply betting on the movements of the market, for a brief moment in some cases, for as long as several months in others.

A summary of a recent day's trading appears as Figure 9.2. In addition to trading in the S&P 500, there are less active markets in other stock indexes. Several contracts on the S&P 500 trade at the same time, for future delivery in June, September, December, and March. The value of each contract is defined as $500 times the level of the index, which, at 180, would equal $90,000. Margin requirements are often in the $6,000–$9,000 range, so the leverage for gains and losses is quite large here also. The futures contracts tend to move with the S&P 500 index itself, and large institutional arbitrageurs see to it that this is so. If the futures price rises too far above the level of the index itself, the "big hitters" can buy the underlying S&P 500 stocks, or a good sample of them, and simultaneously sell the futures contracts, making a profit with very little risk, since at expiration the futures contract price must equal the S&P 500 index. If the futures price falls below the "cash" or actual level of the S&P 500 index, institutions can buy the futures and sell the S&P 500 stocks, again guaranteeing a riskless profit.*

While this market gives a player a chance to make daily or hourly bets on the market, I do not recommend it for PAD investors. The leverage is too great, so that small and random fluctuations can wipe out your capital very quickly, even if you have guessed right about the direction of the market. In addition, as I pointed out in Chapter 7, the day-to-day fluctuations in the market are so close to being random that it should be almost impossible to outguess the market consistently on a short-term basis.

An even more serious problem with these markets is that they may be subject to short-term manipulation by large investors, which will almost certainly be to the detriment of most small speculators. This possibility became apparent in 1985, when the simultaneous expiration of a variety of options periodically led to violent and otherwise inexplicable movements in both stock and futures markets. Rumors periodically surface about

---

*This "program trading" seems to make stock prices more volatile on some days, but I doubt there are any long-term effects.

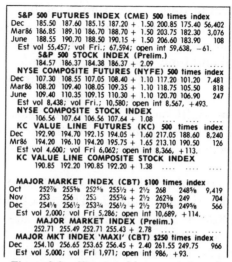

S&P 500 FUTURES INDEX (CME) 500 times index								
Dec	185.50	187.60	185.15	187.20	+ 1.50	200.85	175.40	56,402
Mar86	186.85	189.10	186.70	188.70	+ 1.50	203.75	182.30	3,076
June	188.55	190.70	188.50	190.15	+ 1.50	206.60	183.90	108
Est vol 55,457; vol Fri.; 67,594; open int 59,638, −61.								
S&P 500 STOCK INDEX (Prelim.)								
	184.57	186.37	184.38	186.37	+ 2.09	....	....	....
NYSE COMPOSITE FUTURES (NYFE) 500 times index								
Dec	107.30	108.55	107.05	108.40	+ 1.10	117.20	101.20	7,481
Mar86	108.20	109.40	108.05	109.35	+ 1.10	118.75	105.50	818
June	109.40	110.35	109.15	110.30	+ 1.10	120.70	106.90	247
Est vol 8,438; vol Fri.; 10,580; open int 8,567, +493.								
NYSE COMPOSITE STOCK INDEX								
	106.56	107.64	106.56	107.64	+ 1.08	....	....	....
KC VALUE LINE FUTURES (KC) 500 times index								
Dec	192.90	194.70	192.15	194.05	+ 1.60	217.05	188.60	8,240
Mr86	194.20	196.10	194.20	195.75	+ 1.65	213.10	190.50	126
Est vol 4,600; vol Fri 6,062; open int 8,366, +113.								
KC VALUE LINE COMPOSITE STOCK INDEX								
	190.85	192.20	190.85	192.20	+ 1.38	....	....	....
MAJOR MARKET INDEX (CBT) $100 times index								
Oct	252 7/8	255 5/8	252 5/8	255 1/2	+ 2 1/2	268	248 5/8	9,419
Nov	253	256	253	255 3/4	+ 2 1/2	262 3/8	249	704
Dec	254 1/8	256 1/2	253 3/4	256 1/2	+ 2 1/2	270 5/8	249 5/8	566
Est vol 2,000; vol Fri 5,286; open int 10,689, +114.								
MAJOR MARKET INDEX (Prelim.)								
	252.71	255.49	252.71	255.43	+ 2.78	....	....	....
MAJOR MKT INDEX 'MAXI' (CBT) $250 times index								
Dec	254.10	256.65	253.65	256.45	+ 2.40	261.55	249.75	966
Est vol 5,000; vol Fri 1,971; open int 986, +93.								

Figure 9.2 (Reprinted by permission of the *Wall Street Journal* © Dow Jones & Company, Inc., 1985. All rights reserved.)

new manipulation schemes for stocks, futures, and options. Some of these rumors are probably true, and thus the ordinary investor must be even more wary of playing the short-term speculation game.

C. OPTIONS ON STOCK INDEX FUTURES

The CME and other major exchanges have created markets in options on the stock index futures discussed in the preceding section. The most active market is again for options on the S&P 500, and I will discuss them exclusively in this section.

With the operations of the stock options markets discussed in Section A in mind, it is only a short mental step to understanding options on S&P 500 futures. Let's look at call options first. The buyer of a call option has the right to purchase an S&P 500 futures contract at a specified (striking) price for a specified period of time, i.e., until the expiration date. The writer of the call option must deliver if requested (called). The options themselves have a value that fluctuates from day to day just as other kinds of options do. The fluctuations are tied to fluctuations in futures prices, which are tied to fluctuations in the S&P index itself. An example will help illustrate how this works. Suppose it is April and the S&P 500 index stands at 200. Based on recent experience, the June S&P 500 futures contract will trade at a price higher than this in April, say at 203. Then the June call option on the S&P 500 with a striking price of 200 will sell for

at least 3, its intrinsic value, since it gives the buyer the right to buy
something for 3 less than the market price right now. Let's say it sells for
5 (2 points time value), reflecting the possibility that the S&P 500 could
rise between April and June, making large profits for the option holder.
Since the option buyer has a potential loss limited to the size of the option
payment, he or she is willing to pay more than the current intrinsic value
for the option. This additional payment for time value depends on several
factors, including the time remaining before the option expires. (This was
also the case in Section A.) In general, the time value will fall as expiration approaches.

Now suppose that the S&P 500 rises to 210 in May. Then the June
future will probably rise to about 212. (The size of this premium is also
slowly shrinking toward zero at expiration.) The 200 call option is now
worth at least 12, since it gives the holder the right to buy something for
200 which is worth 212 in the open market. It will thus have its own additional time value, again reflecting time remaining to expiration and the
market sentiments of options writers and buyers. If the time value is 1,
then the price of the option is now 13 (12 + 1). The 10-point rise in the
S&P 500 is equivalent to a 5 percent gain over the month, while the value
of the option has risen from 5 to 13, a gain of 160 percent. These numbers
are arranged for easy reference in Table 9.1. The gain on the futures contract is also substantial and, depending on the particular circumstances,
could be as large or larger in percentage terms than the options gain. The
crucial difference between the two is that the futures contract entails virtually unlimited potential for loss, while the option has a loss limited to
the price paid for the option. This limited loss, coupled with the potential for enormous leveraged gains, shows again why options buyers will
pay more than the intrinsic value for an option at any time until expiration.

TABLE 9.1   Call Options and Futures: A Market Advance

Trade/Month	April	May	% Change
(1) S&P 500	200	210	+5%
(2) S&P 500 future	203 (buy)	212 (sell)	+4.5 to +100%*
(3) June 200 call	5 (buy)	13 (sell)	+160%

*High figures assume high margin leverage ($4,500 margin per contract) and no margin
calls.

The call option buyer must face up to the possibility that the market
may not rise between April and May or June. Suppose that the S&P 500
stays at 200 for the months of May and June. Then at expiration, the June

futures price will equal the "cash" price of 200. A call option with a striking price of 200 will accordingly expire worthless, since no one will pay
for the right to buy a futures contract for 200 when it can be bought for
200 in the open market, and the option is in the process of expiring.
Table 9.2 lays out the grim results: the holder of a diversified portfolio
that tracks the S&P 500 will break even over the period, while the holders
of futures contracts and options will lose. In this case the options player
will suffer a 100 percent loss, which is greater than the loss suffered by
the futures player here.

TABLE 9.2   Call Options and Futures: No Change in Market

Trade/Month	April	June	% Change
(1) S&P 500	200	200	0
(2) S&P 500 future	203 (buy)	200 (sell)	− 1.5 to − 35% *
(3) June 200 call	5 (buy)	0 (sell)	− 100%

*High figures assume high margin leverage ($4,500 margin per contract) and no margin
calls.

   Writers of call options may be futures traders who have bought futures
contracts in anticipation of a market rally. They can write calls against
their holdings just as in the stock option example in Section A. Other writers
may be writing "naked" calls, again with no limit on the extent of loss.
Still other writers may be involved in complex forms of arbitrage that will
not concern us here.
   Once a call buyer has turned bearish on the market and sold his or
her calls to someone else in the market, it is quite simple to "switch gears"
and buy put options on the S&P 500 futures in order to profit from a stock
market decline. Again, suppose that in April the S&P 500 is 200, and the
June futures contract is trading for 203. Then a put option with a striking
price of 205 must sell for at least 2, its intrinsic value, since it gives the
holder the right to sell something at 205 which can be bought in the open
market for 203. This option will also have time value, say, 2 points (for
a total price of 4), since buyers will again pay for the privilege of a levered
bet with limited loss. Now suppose that the market indeed declines in May,
with the S&P 500 falling to 190. Then the June futures will probably still
trade higher than the cash price, but the premium may have fallen to 2,
so that the futures price will be 192. Using the same reasoning as before,
the put option with a striking price of 205 is worth at least 13, and if the
time value is 1, reflecting the reduction in time remaining until expiration, the put option will sell for 14. Thus, the put buyer has more than

tripled his or her money and the seller of a futures contract has also done well, whereas the holder of the S&P 500 has suffered a loss of 5 percent. These details are spelled out in Table 9.3.

TABLE 9.3 Put Options and Futures: A Market Decline

Trade/Month	April	May	% Change
(1) S&P 500	200	190	−5%
(2) S&P 500 future	203 (sell)	192 (buy)	+4.5 to +100%*
(3) June 205 put	4 (buy)	14 (sell)	+250%

*High figures assume high margin leverage ($4,500 margin per contract) and no margin calls.

The put buyer must also be prepared for the possibility of loss if the market rises instead of falling. For example, if the market rises to 210, an increase of 5 percent, by the end of June, the put buyer will see the value of a 205 put decline to zero, since at expiration no one will pay for the right to sell something at 205 which can be sold in the open market for 210. In this case the put buyer loses 100 percent of his or her investment and the seller of a futures contract loses heavily also, whereas our staid stockholder makes 5 percent. The bad news is summarized in Table 9.4.

TABLE 9.4 Put Options and Futures: A Market Advance

Trade/Month	April	June	% Change
(1) S&P 500	200	210	+5%
(2) S&P 500 future	203 (sell)	210 (buy)	−3.5 to −80%*
(3) June 205 put	4 (buy)	0 (sell)	−100%

*High figures assume high margin leverage ($4,500 margin per contract) and no margin calls.

An example of actual call and put option prices is reprinted from the *Wall Street Journal* in Figure 9.3. (These prices appear on or near the futures prices page of the second section of the paper.) On the day shown in October 1985, the S&P 500 index closed at 186.37, and the December future closed at 187.20. The futures options market was fairly active, with about 3,000 options contracts changing hands. Striking prices are listed down the left side of the table, followed by call option prices and then put option prices, arrayed by expiration date, with the December prices, the nearest, listed first. Prices listed are the closing prices of the

FUTURES OPTIONS

Monday, October 14, 1985.

- AGRICULTURAL -

CORN (CBT) 5,000 bu.; cents per bu.

Strike Price	Calls–Settle Dec-C	Mar-C	May-C	Puts–Settle Dec-P	Mar-P	May-P
2.00	22½	....	....	¼	⅜	....
2.10	12½	24¾	....	½	¾	1
2.20	5¼	16½	....	2⅝	2¼	2
2.30	1⅜	10¼	15½	8½	5½	5¾
2.40	¼	5⅜	9¾	17½	10½	10
2.50	⅛	2½	6	27½	17	15

Est. vol. 1,000; Fri vol. 952 calls; 543 puts
Open interest Fri; 33,834 calls; 20,850 puts

SOYBEANS (CBT) 5,000 bu.; cents per bu.

Strike Price	Calls–Settle Jan-C	Mar-C	May-C	Puts–Settle Jan-P	Mar-P	May-P
475	....	....	....	1⅛	2	2¾
500	21¾	34	44	5½	6	7½
525	8	18¼	28	16½	14¼	15
550	2⅝	8¼	17	36	29	27
575	⅞	3¾	9½	59	48½	....
600	⅛	1¾	5⅝	83¾	....	....

Est. vol. 1,500; Fri vol. 1,509 calls; 1,700 puts
Open interest Fri; 13,455 calls; 5,800 puts

COTTON (CTN) 50,000 lbs.; cents per lb.

Strike Price	Calls–Settle Dec-C	Mar-C	May-C	Puts–Settle Dec-P	Mar-P	May-P
58	2.10	3.20	....	.13	.60	....
59	1.40	2.50	2.80	.35	.90	.70
60	.70	1.85	2.15	.73	1.15	1.05
61	.32	1.30	1.70	1.35	1.50	1.45
62	.17	1.05	1.20	2.10	2.10	1.80
63	.07	.70	1.05	3.10	2.90	2.30

Est. vol. 100; Fri vol. 21 calls; 18 puts
Open interest Fri; 3,505 calls; 1,755 puts

SUGAR–WORLD (CSCE)–112,000 lbs.; cents per lb.

Strike Price	Calls–Settle Mar-C May-C Jly-C	Puts–Settle Mar-P May-P Jly-P

EXCHANGE CLOSED FOR HOLIDAY Est. vol. ; vol. calls; puts
Open interest ; calls; puts

CATTLE-LIVE (CME) 40,000 lbs.; cents per lb.

T-NOTES (CBT) $ 100,000; points and 64ths of 100%

Strike Price	Calls–Last Dec-C	Mar-C	Jun-C	Puts–Last Dec-P	Mar-P	Jun-P
82	3-47	....	....	0-05	0-46	....
84	1-63	....	....	0-18	1-27	....
86	0-46	1-10	....	1-01	2-30	....
88	0-10	0-38	....	2-30	....	....
90	0-02	0-17	....	....	....	....
92	0-01	....	....	....	....	....

Est. vol. 200, Fri vol. 1,998 calls, 297 puts
Open interest Friday ; 8,536 calls, 4,554 puts

EURODOLLAR (CME) $ million; pts. of 100 %

Strike Price	Calls–Settle Dec-C	Mar-C	Jun-C	Puts–Settle Dec-P	Mar-P	Jun-P
9050	1.14	0.92	0.80	0.02	0.18	0.43
9100	0.68	0.58	0.54	0.05	0.32	0.64
9150	0.31	0.31	0.33	0.17	0.55	0.89
9200	0.09	0.16	0.18	0.45	0.86	1.21
9250	0.02	0.07	....	0.87	1.27	....
9300	0.01	....	....	1.36	....	....

Est. vol. 285, Fri.; vol. 1,256 calls, 1,543 puts
Open interest Fri.; 17,006 calls, 27,438 puts

NYSE COMPOSITE INDEX (NYFE) $500 times premium

Strike Price	Calls–Settle Dec-C	Mar-C	Jun-C	Puts–Settle Dec-P	Mar-P	Jun-P
104	4.90	6.30	7.45	0.50	1.05	1.35
106	3.40	4.90	6.10	1.00	1.60	1.90
108	2.20	3.70	4.90	1.80	2.35	2.60
110	1.35	2.70	3.85	2.95	3.30	3.50
112	0.75	1.90	2.95	4.35	4.50	4.55
114	0.35	1.30	2.25	5.95	5.85	5.80

Est. vol. 285, Fri.; vol. 161 calls, 108 puts
Open interest Fri.; 3,733 calls, 2,986 puts

S&P 500 STOCK INDEX (CME) $500 times premium.

Strike Price	Calls–Settle Dec-C	Mar-C	Jn-C	Puts–Settle Dec-P	Mar-P	Jun-P
180	8.30	10.70	....	1.20	2.30	2.90
185	4.80	7.45	....	2.65	3.85	4.50
190	2.45	4.90	6.80	5.20	6.15	6.65
195	1.10	3.05	4.75	8.75	9.15	....
200	0.50	1.80	3.25	13.10	....	....
205	0.20	1.05	....	....	....	....

Est. vol. 3,030; Fri.; vol. 1,376 calls; 1,299 puts
Open interest Fri.; 16,497 calls; 21,948 puts

Figure 9.3 (Reprinted by permission of the *Wall Street Journal* © Dow Jones & Company, Inc., 1985. All rights reserved.)

day, as determined by the exchange, and are called settlement prices. Thus, the table tells us nothing about the range of prices during the day, or even if there was a range of prices quoted at the closing bell. Looking at the calls first, we see that calls with higher striking prices have lower prices, since the opportunities for gain are less likely. All of the calls above 185 are out-of-the-money calls with no intrinsic value. Notice also that the more life, or time remaining to expiration, a call option has, the higher the price is. Thus, March calls are dearer than December calls, and Junes are dearer still. No settlement price is recorded for options that did not trade. The actual cost of the December 185 call can be easily calculated by multiplying the price by $500. On the day shown, one of these calls will cost almost $2,500 (4.80 × $500 = $2,400). Options that are far out-of-the-money are much cheaper, but the chances that they will increase greatly in value are slim. Hence, the December 205 call costs only

$100 (0.20 × $500), but if the market does not rise above 205 before the end of December, it will expire worthless.

Looking at the put side of the table, we again see that the prices are higher for the options with later expirations. But for put options, the options with the higher striking prices are dearer than the others, since a put is the right to sell. Like the December 185 call, the December 190 put can also be purchased for around $2,500 (5.20 × $500 = $2,600). Costs of the other options can be calculated accordingly. A discount commodities broker will probably charge a commission between $16 and $50 for the purchase and sale of one of these options.

To summarize the examples of this section, the buyers of put and call options on S&P 500 futures (or other stock index futures) can make a leveraged bet on the movement of the stock market with losses limited to the price of the option purchased. Call buyers are betting on rising prices, and put buyers are betting the reverse. This strategy of playing the market is superior to playing the futures themselves, in which losses are not limited to the initial investment. These option bets on the market are offered by option writers, who gain the price paid for the option, in exchange for the chance to make large profits. Yet these market bets are not solely bets on the market, since the prices of puts and calls are tied to the futures prices, not to the underlying index. If the size of the futures premium changes, the prices of the options will change, even if the S&P 500 index remains unchanged. In addition, since the futures premium is usually positive and often equal to several points, the prices of call and put options are distorted when compared to the S&P 500 index itself. Using the newspaper quotations of Figure 9.3, the December 185 call has an intrinsic value, based on the actual S&P 500 or "cash" index, of 1.37 (186.37 − 185 = 1.37), and thus the time value is 3.43 (4.80 − 1.37 = 3.43). The December 190 put option has an intrinsic value, based on the cash index, of 3.63 (190 − 186.37 = 3.63), and thus its time value is only 1.57 (5.20 − 3.63 = 1.57). Thus, the fact that the futures price is higher than the cash price increases call option prices relative to put option prices. Since most of the public is bullish most of the time, and therefore more interested in calls than puts, this is a significant market anomaly.*

For PAD investors, who will use the put options for insurance (see Section E), cheaper puts are a boon. In order to satisfy the public, how-

---

*Readers familiar with Chapter 7 may wonder if this is an example of an exploitable inefficiency. I believe it is, but the strategy to exploit it is extremely complex, involving multiple intermarket spreads.

ever, an even newer type of option was created, called an index option. These index options, as opposed to futures options, have become one of the most popular new financial instruments ever created. It is to these that we now turn.

D. OPTIONS WITHOUT FUTURES: INDEX OPTIONS

A new index was created by Standard and Poor's and the CBOE to serve as the basis for index option trading on the CBOE. Called the S&P 100 index, it is composed of 100 of the 500 S&P stocks in the S&P 500. These stocks were chosen in part to make the 100 index follow the movements of the 500 as closely as possible, while giving small investors a chance to place their bets with smaller stakes: the value of a 100 option is only $100 times the option price, or one-fifth the cost of a 500 option. In addition, the options expirations are set for one, two, and three months from the current month every month, so that on the same date as our S&P 500 example, S&P 100 options were trading for October, November, and December expirations. Both of these differences from the S&P 500 futures options are designed to make option prices affordable for the small investor. The third key difference also makes the prices of call options more affordable: there is no linked futures trading in the S&P 100, which could distort the prices of the options in the manner explained in Section D. Since the call option buyer is not buying the right to buy a futures contract, what is he or she buying? In effect, one buys the right to "buy" the S&P 100 index at expiration, since when trading stops, all options accounts are settled in cash and the options then have only intrinsic value. Before expiration, the price of each option will reflect its intrinsic value, if any, and a time value for the leveraged bet of the option. But the premium of a futures contract over the cash value has been eliminated, which makes the call options cheaper and the put options more expensive. These changes in the contract specifications have made the S&P 100 options so popular that volume often exceeds 400,000 contracts in a single day, and the open interest, or number of contracts outstanding at the end of the day, often exceeds 1,000,000. This success has bred imitation, so that most other exchanges have instituted index option trading. Index options like the S&P 100 have finally given the small investor or speculator the chance to bet on the market for small stakes. Critics of this trading explosion have argued just that: what economic purpose is served by legalizing pure gambling on the stock market? I would not deny that much of this trading is pure gambling, but the nation now tolerates and even encourages gambling on state lotteries. Remember also that commodity futures have an economic function: to spread the risk of price fluctuation, allowing market participants to "hedge" against an uncertain future. Yet a buyer of February pork bellies may be strictly interested in a one-day gamble on the price of pork bellies. In the same manner, stock index futures and options and index options can provide insurance to investors large and small, as well as opportunities for pure gambling. I recommend that PAD investors use these markets solely for insurance rather than gambling, and I explain the insurance technique in Section E.

E. PUT OPTIONS AS INSURANCE: A CONSERVATIVE STRATEGY

We have already seen that put options increase in value when the underlying stock or index declines in value. This insurance aspect of options can be used by the PAD investor to protect a PAD portfolio against a decline in value. If we knew exactly when the market was going to reach a cyclical peak, it would be easy to liquidate all our stocks at the appropriate moment. To paraphrase an old Wall Street adage, "No one rings a bell when the market reaches a top." The phased liquidation of Chapter 3, combined with the timing rules of Chapter 4, will help you liquidate gradually when stocks are no longer cheap. But the market may continue to rise after you have liquidated all of the stocks that meet the rules for a general selling program. If you justifiably fear a temporary but sharp decline in the market, it may be more profitable to buy insurance on your remaining portfolio, rather than liquidate stocks that are still "buys" based on the PAD rules, since these stocks should do well in a raging bull market. If the general public ever returned to the equity markets in full force, stocks could be driven up to valuation levels not seen since the late 1960s. A PAD investor would not want to miss out on this opportunity to sell stock to the unsuspecting public at outrageous prices. In addition to building up cash reserves, the PAD investor can buy insurance to protect his remaining investments while the market is surging upward on unbridled optimism.

There are several ways to "buy" the insurance you need. I recommend buying S&P 500 puts, which tend to have smaller premiums than S&P 100 puts. But the 500s are more costly, so this insurance makes sense only if you have a very large portfolio ($100,000 or more.) In the following example, we assume that your portfolio is worth $200,000. If your portfolio has not reached this loftly level yet, but is in the $20,000–$100,000

CASE HISTORY: S&P 500 PUT OPTIONS

In the spring of 1983, the stock market was clearly overvalued by the standards of Chapter 4. The "Wall Street Week" elves were bearish, and the Value Line median appreciation potential had fallen below 75 percent. Many PAD stocks were trading above the low end of their 3–5 year appreciation potentials.

I sold stocks on my Sell List throughout the first half of 1983, and also decided to purchase put insurance for my remaining portfolio. In March of 1983, with the S&P 500 at 150, I bought two S&P 500 June 150 put options, which expired almost worthless. Gains in my portfolio more than offset this loss, however. I "rolled over" my position into September, December, and March 1984, taking small losses each time. My June 1984 options, however, rose substantially in value before expiration as the market finally began falling in earnest in the spring of 1984. This increase in option value offset some of the loss on my portfolio during the 1984 market decline.

---

range, you can use S&P 100 put options to achieve the same result. Necessaiy modifications to the method are discussed at the end of the example. To add a touch of excitement, let's assume that it is now July, 1990 and the Dow-Jones is hovering around 3,000, the S&P 500 is at 400, the Value Line MAP indicator is at 10 percent, the "Wall Street Week" elves are bearish, and you have liquidated half of your portfolio at a very large profit. It is quite possible that the market will continue on up to 4,000, but you feel it is now time to insure your remaining portfolio against a 500-point correction in the Dow, which would take some of the froth out of the market and some of the value out of your portfolio. Suppose the September S&P 500 futures are trading at 403, and a September 405 option on them is trading at 8 (2 points intrinsic value + 6 points time value). Each option would then cost $4,000. The number of options to buy depends on the amount of portfolio protection you want to buy. Suppose the market declines by 10 percent before September. If the S&P 500 falls to 360, a 10 percent decline, your stocks, which generally rise and fall faster than the broad market averages, may fall in value from $200,000 to (say) $160,000. This $40,000 loss in your portfolio will be partly offset by the increase in the value of your put option, which will be worth about 40 points more, its exact value depending on the size of the futures premium and the option's time value. This 40 points is worth $20,000, and thus your overall loss has been halved. Hence, one put option on the S&P 500 has given you 50 percent insurance protection. If you purchased two options, you would then have approximately 100 percent protection. Of course, if the market continues to rise, the value of your put option(s) will fall, and your put(s) may expire worthless. But the value of your portfolio will also rise, and it is likely that it will rise faster than the value of your put option(s) will fall. The situation is analogous to homeowner's insurance: you do not get your insurance premium back just because your house did not burn down!

It may also happen that the stock market remains flat between July and September. In this case your put option will decline in value slowly but, in the example here, will still have some value near expiration. (If you still fear a market decline, you can "roll over" your put insurance as explained in the Appendix.) This residual value of your option is not unlike a policy dividend. Unfortunately, the insurance analogy breaks down at this point. If you had purchased a 400 put instead, which was cheaper since it had no intrinsic value, it would expire worthless and there would be no "dividend."

We have made a crucial assumption in this example that your stocks will follow the direction of the market. This is not always a safe assumption, since high-technology stocks fall out of favor with investors periodically (as do most stock groups), and when these stocks are "in the doghouse," the market could rise while high-tech portfolios lose ground. In this worst of all possible cases, your option insurance will decline in value at the same time that your stocks decline in value, so that the insurance role of the put will have been destroyed by this divergence in performance.* It is more likely, however, that high-technology stocks will lead a raging bull market, rather than be left behind. And it is during a raging bull market that a PAD investor is likely to turn to put options for insurance.

Let me review the key elements of this section. When, during a bull market, the PAD investor has completed a selling program in accordance with the rules of Chapters 2–4, and wishes to protect his or her remaining portfolio stocks against a sharp market decline, put options on the S&P 100 or the S&P 500 futures can be purchased as insurance. Up to 100 percent "coverage" can be obtained, although the insurance will not "pay off" if your portfolio declines while the general market rises. (If the

---

*Subindex options could solve the problem, but technology subindex options trading is much too thin.

market falls while your portfolio increases in value, you of course receive an extra dividend.)

For the smaller PAD investor, insurance can be purchased by buying put options on the S&P 100 index. These options are ⅕ the size of the S&P 500 options, so insurance can be purchased in smaller amounts. The expiration months are arranged differently than the 500, however, with no option trading with more than three months until expiration. A December option on the S&P 100 could be purchased as in the example above, and its price will be tied to the S&P 100 index, which follows the broad movements of the S&P 500, although there are frequent divergences between the two. Over the short history of the S&P 100, it has traded at the same level as the 500 and as much as 14 index points below it. Again, the protection you actually get will depend on how closely your portfolio tracks the movements of the S&P 100. Your S&P 100 puts will expire worthless if the market and the 100 index rise; and if your stocks fall instead of following the market, you can lose on your portfolio too. Again, while this is unlikely, it is not at all impossible.

GLOSSARY OF TERMS

Bid–ask spread   The difference between the buying (ask) and selling (bid) prices for an option.

Call option   The right to buy the underlying security, index, or index future.

Cash price   The current level of the stock index itself.

Covered option writing   Writing (selling) of options on stocks or futures contracts you own.

Expiration date   The last day of trading for an option or future.

Futures   Contracts for future delivery of a commodity or financial asset of some kind, including a stock index.

Futures option   The right to buy or sell a futures contract until the expiration date.

Index futures   Futures traded on stock indexes.

Index options   Options on stock indexes in which settlement is in cash rather than in stock index futures.

"In-the-money" option   An option that has intrinsic value, that is, a call option with a striking price below the market price or a put option with a striking price above the market price.

Intrinsic value   What an option is worth if exercised.

Leverage   Any technique that increases the magnitudes of gains and losses.

Naked option writing   Writing a call option without owning the underlying stock, or writing a put option without holding a short position in the underlying stock.

"Out-of-the-money" option   A call option with a striking price above the market price or a put option with a striking price below the market price.

Premium   Total payment for an option, composed of intrinsic value and time value.

Put option   The right to sell the underlying stock, index, or future.

Spot price   Another term for cash price.

Striking price   The price at which an option can be exercised.

Time value   Any premium in excess of intrinsic value.

Readings for the PAD Investor

JOHN COX AND MARK RUBINSTEIN, *Options Markets*. Englewood Cliffs NJ.: Prentice-Hall, 1985. A thorough and well-written book. For those with training in finance or economics.

LIN TSO, *Complete Investors Guide to Listed Options: Calls and Puts*. Englewood Cliffs NJ.: Prentice-Hall, 1981. Somewhat dated, but a good practical guide for the novice.

"Understanding the Risks and Uses of Listed Options." A booklet prepared jointly by the major exchanges. Published October 1982. An introduction to the basics.

"Listed Options on Stock Indices." Another booklet prepared jointly by the major exchanges. Published March 1983. More of the basics.

APPENDIX: "ROLLING OVER" PUT OPTIONS

A PAD investor with a portfolio large enough to use the S&P 500 options as insurance can further reduce costs by buying put options with more distant expiration dates. Costs are reduced because the prices of put options on the S&P 500 do not rise in straight-line fashion with time remaining until expiration. This can be clearly seen in Figure 9A.1, which is a reproduction of Figure 9.3. In the figure, the December 190 put option settled at 5.20 for the day, with the S&P cash index at 186.37. If you pur-

FUTURES OPTIONS

Monday, October 14, 1985.

-AGRICULTURAL-

CORN (CBT) 5,000 bu.; cents per bu.

Strike	Calls–Settle			Puts–Settle		
Price	Dec-C	Mar-C	May-C	Dec-P	Mar-P	May-P
2.00	22½	....	....	¼	⅜	....
2.10	12½	24¾	....	½	¾	1
2.20	5¼	16½	....	2⅝	2¼	2
2.30	1⅜	10¼	15½	8½	5½	5¾
2.40	¼	5⅜	9¾	17½	10½	10
2.50	⅛	2½	6	27½	17	15

Est. vol. 1,000; Fri vol. 952 calls; 543 puts
Open interest Fri; 33,834 calls; 20,850 puts

SOYBEANS (CBT) 5,000 bu.; cents per bu.

Strike	Calls–Settle			Puts–Settle		
Price	Jan-C	Mar-C	May-C	Jan-P	Mar-P	May-P
475	....	....	....	1⅛	2	2¾
500	21¾	34	44	5½	6	7½
525	8	18¼	28	16½	14¼	15
550	2⅝	8¼	17	36	29	27
575	⅞	3¾	9½	59	48½	....
600	⅛	1¾	5⅜	83¾	....	....

Est. vol. 1,500; Fri vol. 1,509 calls; 1,700 puts
Open interest Fri; 13,455 calls; 5,800 puts

COTTON (CTN) 50,000 lbs.; cents per lb.

Strike	Calls–Settle			Puts–Settle		
Price	Dec-C	Mar-C	May-C	Dec-P	Mar-P	May-P
58	2.10	3.20	....	.13	.60	....
59	1.40	2.50	2.80	.35	.90	.70
60	.70	1.85	2.15	.73	1.15	1.05
61	.32	1.30	1.70	1.35	1.50	1.45
62	.17	1.05	1.20	2.10	2.10	1.80
63	.07	.70	1.05	3.10	2.90	2.30

Est. vol. 100; Fri vol. 21 calls; 18 puts
Open interest Fri; 3,505 calls; 1,755 puts

SUGAR–WORLD (CSCE)–112,000 lbs.; cents per lb.

Strike	Calls–Settle			Puts–Settle		
Price	Mar-C	May-C	Jly-C	Mar-P	May-P	Jly-P

EXCHANGE CLOSED FOR HOLIDAY Est. vol. ; vol. calls; puts
Open interest ; calls; puts

CATTLE-LIVE (CME) 40,000 lbs.; cents per lb.

T-NOTES (CBT) $ 100,000; points and 64ths of 100%

Strike	Calls–Last			Puts–Last		
Price	Dec-C	Mar-C	Jun-C	Dec-P	Mar-P	Jun-P
82	3-47	....	....	0-05	0-46	....
84	1-63	....	....	0-18	1-27	....
86	0-46	1-10	....	1-01	2-30	....
88	0-10	0-38	....	2-30	....	....
90	0-02	0-17	....	....	....	....
92	0-01	....	....	....	....	....

Est. vol. 200, Fri vol. 1,998 calls, 297 puts
Open interest Friday ; 8,536 calls, 4,554 puts

EURODOLLAR (CME) $ million; pts. of 100 %

Strike	Calls–Settle			Puts–Settle		
Price	Dec-C	Mar-C	Jun-C	Dec-P	Mar-P	Jun-P
9050	1.14	0.92	0.80	0.02	0.18	0.43
9100	0.68	0.58	0.54	0.05	0.32	0.64
?150	0.31	0.31	0.33	0.17	0.55	0.89
9200	0.09	0.16	0.18	0.45	0.86	1.21
9250	0.02	0.07	....	0.87	1.27	....
9300	0.01	....	....	1.36	....	....

Est. vol. 285, Fri.; vol. 1,256 calls, 1,543 puts
Open interest Fri.; 17,006 calls, 27,438 puts

NYSE COMPOSITE INDEX (NYFE) $500 times premium

Strike	Calls–Settle			Puts–Settle		
Price	Dec-C	Mar-C	Jun-C	Dec-P	Mar-P	Jun-P
104	4.90	6.30	7.45	0.50	1.05	1.35
106	3.40	4.90	6.10	1.00	1.60	1.90
108	2.20	3.70	4.90	1.80	2.35	2.60
110	1.35	2.70	3.85	2.95	3.30	3.50
112	0.75	1.90	2.95	4.35	4.50	4.55
114	0.35	1.30	2.25	5.95	5.85	5.80

Est. vol. 285, Fri.; vol. 161 calls, 108 puts
Open interest Fri.; 3,733 calls, 2,986 puts

S&P 500 STOCK INDEX (CME) $500 times premium.

Strike	Calls–Settle			Puts–Settle		
Price	Dec-C	Mar-C	Jn-C	Dec-P	Mar-P	Jun-P
180	8.30	10.70	....	1.20	2.30	2.90
185	4.80	7.45	....	2.65	3.85	4.50
190	2.45	4.90	6.80	5.20	6.15	6.65
195	1.10	3.05	4.75	8.75	9.15	....
200	0.50	1.80	3.25	13.10	....	....
205	0.20	1.05	....	....	....	....

Est. vol. 3,030; Fri.; vol. 1,376 calls; 1,299 puts
Open interest Fri.; 16,497 calls; 21,948 puts

Figure 9.A.1 (Reprinted by permission of the *Wall Street Journal* © Dow Jones & Company, Inc., 1985. All rights reserved.)

chased this option as insurance, and the market remained flat until expiration in late December, the option would expire at 3.63, its intrinsic value. The "cost" of your insurance is the loss you would take on your options position, which is 5.20 − 3.63 = 1.57 points, where each point equals $500. If, instead, you purchased a March 190 put option, you would pay 6.15 points for it initially, based on Figure 9A.1 prices. If you also held it until the expiration of the December option, and if the market remained at 186.37, your option would be worth more than 3.63, since it would still have three months left until expiration. How big would this premium be? A reasonable guess is that a March option in December would be worth at least as much as a December option in October, since each has several months to run at that point. This means that your March option should sell for at least 5.20 come December, with the S&P 500 still at 186.37. (It should actually be worth more than this, since it has longer to run than the December option did.) Your cost has now been reduced to 6.15 − 5.20 = 0.95 points, close to a 50 percent reduction compared to the previous example.

This saving in your insurance premiums could not be further reduced by purchasing the still more remote June option, because in 1985, this market was too thinly traded to provide sufficient liquidity for buyers to enter or exit the market without having a significant impact upon prices. (The proof of this point would depend on the bid–ask spread for the more distant option.)

When December arrives and, in your opinion, the market is still vulnerable to a steep drop, you can acquire inexpensive portfolio insurance until March by "rolling over" your option position from the March option to the June option. You should be able to sell your March option in December for 5.20 and buy a June option for 6.15. If the market continues to hover around 186.37 on the S&P 500, you can continue to "roll over" your option position as long as there is a significant danger of a market decline. "Rolling over" and using the more distant option months will provide continuous and inexpensive insurance. Commission costs will be small with a discount commodities broker, and the bid–ask spread should also be small for actively traded options. If the market does decline, your option profits will offset some or all of the losses sustained by your portfolio stocks. If the market rises, your insurance premium will disappear, but this "loss" should be more than offset by gains in your portfolio.

10

ODDS AND ENDS

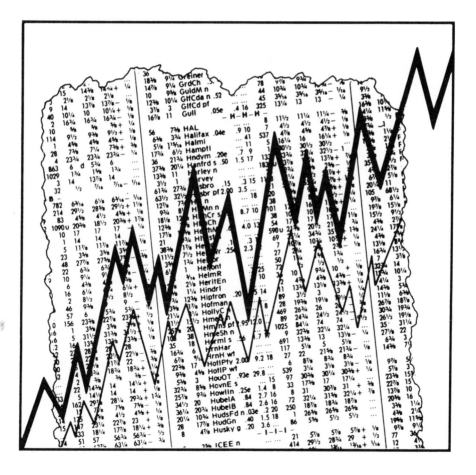

This chapter contains a broad range of advice for PAD investors. There is no particular order to the presentation of topics, and in many cases each topic is an introduction to a complex subject. I suggest the reader browse through those topics that are of special interest or concern. The choices lie among taxes, tax reform, ethical investing, biotechnology, computers and investing, managing information flow, and PAD no-no's (selling short, commodity futures, and Ponzi schemes).

A. TAXES

1. General Strategy

Near the end of every calendar year daily columns on stock market activity often mention "tax-loss selling" as a factor in the market's behavior, and at the very end of the year the end of this selling is also frequently mentioned. In this section I explain the tax-loss selling phenomenon and present a few rules to help you do your buying and selling in a way consistent with keeping your taxes low. The most important lesson of the section, however, is to avoid letting your tax strategy control your portfolio strategy. You can take advantage of stock market bargains created by others who make this mistake.

The 1984 tax law revisions provided a significant incentive to hold onto stock at least six months.* Shares sold within six months of purchase are subject to tax as ordinary income. On the other hand, only 40 percent of the profits on shares held more than six months are subject to tax as ordinary income. Thus, for an investor in the 35 percent tax bracket, that is, someone earning income such that the next dollar they earn will require payment of 35 cents in additional taxes, long-term capital gains are taxed at just 14 percent (.4 × .35), which is an excellent form of tax shelter. The strategies presented in this book will generally lead to long-term profits, which are then taxed at a favorable rate. Short-term losses (and losses are inevitable) can be used to reduce taxable income up to $3,000 in a year, with no limit to the number of years they can be carried forward. Long-term losses also offset income, but at the rate of $2 of loss offsetting $1 of income. Again, there is no time limit on using up a tax-loss carryforward, but I would hope that adherence to the PAD rules will result in the more pleasant problem of paying taxes on gains.

These tax rules encourage many investors to adjust their portfolio strategies for tax purposes. In fact, the pervasiveness of the tax system and its rules drives some individuals to arrange their lives—and even their deaths—so as to minimize taxes. I do not recommend this approach to life or to the stock market. What a PAD investor can do is make slight adjustments to strategy which can reduce taxes or postpone tax payments while maintaining the essential PAD strategy intact.

My first rule is to have a housecleaning of your portfolio at least once a year. This is probably best done at the time of a general review of your portfolio. August is my favorite month, partly because new Value Line reports on the electronics, semiconductor, and computer industries appear in mid-month, and partly because I prefer to do my housecleaning before the majority of investors do theirs. In particular, any stocks on your Sell List, which you are keeping in accordance with the rules of Chapters 2–4, should be sold by the early fall, especially if you have short-term losses, which are worth more than long-term losses. I cannot emphasize too strongly that these sales should be undertaken only because you have decided to "bail out" of a company's stock, not because you "need" tax

---

*This tax-favored holding period is scheduled to revert to one year in 1987, and it is likely that tax reform will reduce or eliminate altogether preferential treatment for capital gains.

losses to offset gains. This latter type of selling is an example of tax strategy ruling portfolio strategy.

If the market timing indicators of Chapter 4 are suggesting that the market is relatively cheap, all of the proceeds from your sales should be reinvested in companies that meet the criteria of Chapter 2. If there are not sufficient stocks that meet the criteria, maintain cash reserves until there are.

2. Sale and Repurchase

If in fact you have not lost confidence in the stock on which you have taken a loss, you can undertake another strategy to reduce current taxes with a short-term loss and perhaps convert future gains to the more favorably taxed long-term variety. Any stock you sell for a tax loss can be repurchased thirty-one days later without the transaction being considered a "wash sale," that is, a transaction undertaken solely to reduce taxes. (Losses on wash sales do not qualify as tax losses.) The main drawback of this approach is that it is always possible that the stock will rise during the thirty-one day waiting period. Thus, I recommend this strategy for only a limited number of stocks, and only when the market is relatively expensive by Chapter 4's standards.

It is also possible, although the commission costs will begin to mount up, to follow more complex strategies that will protect you against a sudden upsurge in your stock while you are counting off the 31 days. The purchase of a call option (see Chapter 9) on your stock can lock in a price at which you can get back into the market. Many stocks still do not have exchange-traded options, and regular use of the options markets for individual stocks requires additional time and expertise which I do not think is necessary for most PAD investors. More importantly, the IRS might conclude that your trading scheme is the equivalent of a wash sale. Only with exquisitely bad timing will a stock you have suffered with for six months or a year explode in the one month you do not own it, especially if your market timing is better than average. In fact, if you houseclean ahead of the pack, you may be able to buy back when others are selling, and repurchase at a price below your sale price.

We can hope that more of your efforts will be devoted to timing the realization of your long-term gains. If you sell stock for a profit at the end of the year, it is possible to defer paying income taxes on the gain for almost 16 months. Capital gains taxes for a sale in the last few days of December are not due until April 15 of the year following the new year.

(Any broker can tell you which trade days call for a settlement date in the following year.) This delayed payment is equivalent to an interest-free loan from the IRS.*

Most investors sell their losers from October through December, so this is not a good time to sell yours. Some stocks on your Buy List may need just a little decline, induced by tax-loss selling, to exceed the 100 per-cent minimum appreciation potential hurdle of Chapter 2. Be prepared.

3. Short-term Gains

A stock that rises rapidly shortly after purchase can also create a dilemma for the PAD investor, especially if the market as a whole appears overvalued. On the one hand, if you continue to hold the stock to qualify for favorable long-term capital-gains treatment, the bubble may burst. On the other, if you sell and pay the full tax rate and the market does not decline, you have paid much more in taxes than necessary with perfect hindsight, of course. Again, one way out of this pleasant predicament is with an option, in this case a put option. (Full details are presented in Chapter 9.) A put option on a stock gives you the right to sell it at a stated price for a fixed period of months. The IRS does not consider the stock sold, however, until you have actually sold the stock to someone, and the option only gives you the right, not a binding contractual obligation, to sell. This right, which will increase in value if the stock price falls, may not be cheap to buy: you must pay the option seller for the privilege, and the broker will charge you a commission. Extra time and learning will be required on your part, and the strategy cannot be applied to those stocks which have no options trading. A put option will provide you with a hedge against a market decline while you wait for your gains to qualify for favorable tax treatment.

A simpler alternative is to sell part of your holdings, lock in the gain, and pay your taxes. If the market does go down while you are waiting for your profit to become long term, you could easily lose more than you would have paid in higher taxes! If you refuse to sell because of the tax consequences, you have begun to let tax strategy rule portfolio strategy, which, I repeat, is a major error. In this example, the danger may be

---

*If you must pay quarterly estimated tax, the value of the tax deferral is not as great, although you pay no penalty if your total tax payments are at least 90 percent of your liability. (This percentage could be changed at any time.) It is also true that you can sell at the end of the year and count the transaction in that year if you prefer.

relatively small, but many investors use the tax argument to justify holding stocks with large capital gains long after they should have been sold.

CASE HISTORIES: TEXAS INSTRUMENTS AND GENRAD
(Figures 10.1 and 10.2)

I was faced with the short-term gain dilemma in 1983 in two stocks: Texas Instruments (TXN), which, with a little luck, I had purchased in August, 1982 at 84. The great bull market carried it to 150 in less than a year and I decided to take my profits, even though they were taxed at the full rate. It did rise to 170 after I sold it, but then the company's failure in home computers drove the stock down to 100. I was happy to get out, and I would consider buying back in at 84!

I had purchased Genrad (GEN) at 12 in the Spring of 1982 and by the Spring of 1983 the same bull market had driven it to 30. I wrestled with the short-term gain problem and decided to sell half of my holding. It subsequently rose to 45 after becoming a long-term gain, but slower earnings growth and the bear market of 1984 dragged it under 20, and mounting losses for the company in 1985 pushed the stock back below 12. I sold the remaining shares at 12, months after it had been downgraded to "5" for short-term performance by Value Line. I broke my own rules and paid the price!

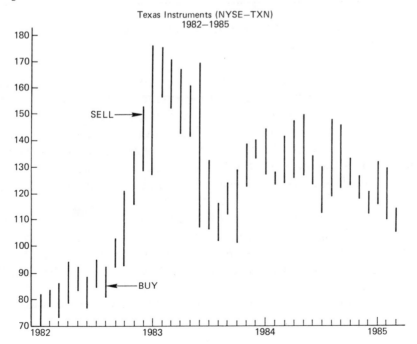

Texas Instruments (NYSE—TXN)
1982–1985

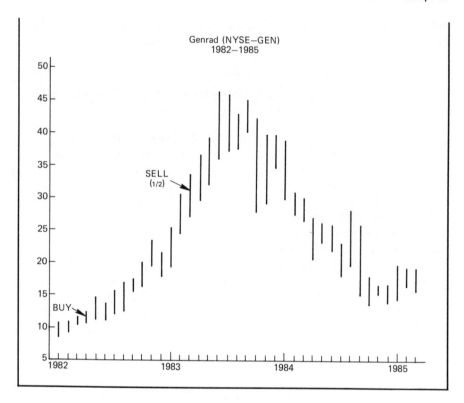

Genrad (NYSE—GEN)
1982—1985

4. Tax Shelters for the PAD Investor: IRAs, Keoghs, etc.

The individual retirement account (IRA) is the best tax break given to the middle class since the home mortgage interest deduction was created. I think everyone should have one, and if your cash flow can tolerate it, contribute the maximum each year.* (The IRA is supposed to encourage saving in the United States, and since we do precious little of that, I consider it one of the more justifiable tax breaks.) You must be extremely patient with IRA money, however, since, under normal conditions, it cannot be withdrawn without penalty before age 59½.

There are several alternatives for managing this money. If you are a full-fledged PAD investor, you can manage it yourself through a discount brokerage firm, but there are fees and commissions to pay, and these can be significant when the account is small. A better alternative for small

---

*Tax reform has eliminated the tax benefit of IRA contributions for some workers.

accounts is to set up an IRA with a no-load mutual fund family that has both a growth stock or technology fund and a cash fund in its family of funds. You can use the market timing techniques of Chapter 4 to switch your money from cash to stock and back, and the costs are generally quite low. Annual IRA fees are very small, and management fees are usually half a percent or less. All dividends and capital gains will be automatically reinvested for you. The switches between funds are usually free, although the number of switches per year may be limited. Some fund families will even let you switch by telephone.

Full-service brokers, who make a substantial commission when they sell customers load mutual funds, may tell clients that no-load mutual funds have an inferior performance record or are not as safe as load mutual funds. There is no evidence that this is true. There are load and no-load funds that have done well and done poorly over every time period ever studied. (As noted in Chapter 7, many academic studies of mutual fund performance have concluded that mutual funds as a group do not pro-vide superior risk-adjusted returns.) I recommend studying the regular performance reviews of mutual funds, which are available in most libraries (many magazines publish ratings also), and deciding on a mutual fund family without benefit of a sales pitch. Self-employed individuals can put money into a Keogh plan at a much faster rate than wage earners can. I would recommend the same strategies for Keogh PAD investors.

Employees of educational institutions, and others who can qualify under section 403b of the tax code, are entitled to pay pretax dollars into a tax-deferred annuity (TDA) plan. The money compounds tax-free until it is withdrawn, but some plans do restrict withdrawal or charge extra fees for premature withdrawal. In many cases, the switching options available are similar to the mutual fund switching option previously mentioned. Annuity firms that allow more flexibility in investments are more desirable, others things being equal. One of the largest, the College Teacher's Retirement Equity Fund (CREF), has historically provided very little flexibility in investments. If you have already put your money into CREF and are unable to get any investment flexibility, you could still pro-tect your CREF holdings against a market decline by purchasing S&P 500 put options, as described in Chapter 9. This could provide an almost perfect hedge, since the CREF portfolio is tied very closely to the S&P 500 index.

I must also point out that these tax shelter plans are only as safe as the underlying insurance company. CREF is quite safe, and so are the largest insurance companies, although nothing is absolutely safe in today's world. Baldwin-United investors discovered the risks involved. Holders

of the firm's single-payment deferred annuities lost much sleep, if not principal and interest, when the company plunged into Chapter 11 bankruptcy
in the mid 1980s.

There are of course many other schemes, legal and otherwise,
designed to reduce taxes. Most of these only make economic sense for the
rich and near-rich. Successful tax reform would eliminate most of these
shelters, which often have no economic function. If you are determined
to invest in oil drilling participations or suburban shopping malls, you
will have no trouble finding assistance. Our tax code has spawned an entire
industry to serve you.

B. TAX REFORM

Many American presidents have tried to reform the American tax
code, often with little success. Everyone wants to see unfair tax breaks
eliminated, except for the ones they use! If we start from first principles
to design a simple and "fair" tax code, we would choose first, a small
number of tax brackets for simplicity; second, progressive tax rates, that
is, higher tax rates for higher incomes; and third, horizontal equity, that
is, equal taxes for equal incomes. The latter two items also give us fairness
and simplicity: poor people would pay no taxes, rich people would pay
plenty of taxes, and those of us in between would pay the same taxes on
a (say) $40,000-a-year income whether the source was wages, capital gains,
interest, or shares of corporate profits. It would not matter how many
children we had, whether we owned our home, gave to charity, or drilled
for oil. This ultimate in simplicity and fairness would save massive ad-
ministrative costs, eliminate all activities designed to shelter income, and
permit us to raise the same dollars from individual income taxes with much
lower marginal tax rates.*

Of course, such a plan will never become law. First, some deductions are "sacred," that is, they have existed for so long and benefit such
a large group that lawmakers will not risk making a change. Home mortgage interest is an excellent example of such a sacred cow. Many others

---

*I have simplified matters for the sake of argument. The costs of earning income
should be deductible even in this system, and knotty problems such as the "marriage
penalty" would still have to be resolved.

are nearly as sacred, and once we agree that some deductions or exemptions are justified on equity or economic grounds, we have opened the door for the "special interests," which include you and me. Tax reform in 1985 followed this pattern. The simplest plans become more complex and less "fair," in order to improve chances of passage into law. I doubt that we can resist using the tax code for social engineering, and thus major reform efforts are doomed to failure. We can hope that minor reforms can be made: eliminating abusive tax shelters, for example.*

There is little reason, then, to plan in advance for major tax reform. Even if investors may discover that the maximum tax rate on capital gains will be raised or lowered a bit, or that maximum contributions to IRAs or other tax plans are increased or reduced, the PAD system will not require modification. If the corporate tax code is modified, which is a stronger possibility, it is quite possible that some high-technology firms will pay lower taxes than before, and even if they do not, the growth I foresee for these companies will swamp any changes in their tax rates. Even if major changes are put in place, Value Line will incorporate them into its long-term projections, and judicious application of the rules of Chapters 2–4 will still enable the PAD investor to select equities that will outperform the market in the long run.

C. ETHICAL INVESTING

A growing number of investors are concerned about the activities of the firms in which they own shares. Rather than simply buy those stocks they think will best meet their monetary objectives, ethical investors refuse to purchase shares in companies whose lines of business or behavior they find ethically unacceptable. Ethical investing is a very personal matter, however, as there is very little in the area that is purely black or white. I define an ethical investor as anyone who has ever managed his or her portfolio on any basis other than maximum monetary gain. Yet ethical investors disagree about which companies should be avoided for ethical reasons. My opinion in this matter is that you should let your conscience be your guide. If the company's business makes you uncomfortable, don't buy the stock. (If your standards are so high that the universe of potential stocks approaches or equals zero, the stock market is not for you!)

I have been an ethical investor for many years, and my concentration on electronics, computers, and instruments is partly a result of my own ethical considerations. I readily admit that the firms of Silicon Valley are far from perfect in behavior. Pollution from high-technology manufacturing has entered some local water supplies, for example. I am willing to live with this peccadillo. Industries I will not invest in include the tobacco and liquor industries, because I think their products do much harm in the world, and because they have done little to control this damage. I also refuse to invest in the defense industry, mainly because I would be overjoyed to see an end to war and the threat of war in the world, and it would be a shame to have the joy of this unlikely event spoiled by an enormous decline in my defense stocks. Evidence of corporate wrongdoing by major defense contractors has served to harden my opinion on these stocks, since I do not choose to own shares of companies whose executives violate the law. My ethics on defense are not absolute: many high-technology firms sell products to the Pentagon either directly or indirectly. I find this tolerable up to the point where the Pentagon has become one of the firm's biggest customers. The percentage of sales to the U.S. government, if significant, is actually reported by Value Line in the same small section of the individual stock report that contains the R&D percentage.

Firms in other industries are also unsuitable for my ethical portfolio for a variety of reasons. For example, my holdings in General Instrument (Chapter 3) made me uncomfortable because gambling became an important indirect source of their revenues. I would not buy the shares of Grolier, Inc. (not a PAD stock) because I was exposed to and disapproved of their door-to-door sales tactics for their encyclopedias. I am sure the reader has his or her own axe to grind with a particular company, and it is relatively painless to indulge yourself and refuse to buy their stock no matter how highly it is recommended by Value Line.

In sum, if you despise the merchants of sin and death, don't buy their stocks. You have not reduced the universe of stocks that much, unless you enforce your guidelines quite rigidly. The stocks of high-technology companies, except for those whose main customer is the U.S. government, are relatively "clean" by generally accepted ethical standards. For further advice on this topic, I would consult the book listed in the Readings section at the end of the chapter.

D. WHY NOT BIOTECHNOLOGY?

Why *not* invest in biotechnology? A fair question. Biotechnology stocks like Genentech, Cetus, and Monoclonal Antibodies, to name a few, invest heavily in research and development, and should grow at rapid rates in the future. They are now producing, and will continue to discover and market, products that will transform human existence as profoundly as the digital computer. They would seem ideal for a PAD investor's portfolio. Yet I have not discussed these companies for two practical reasons. First, none of them was reviewed by the Value Line Investment Survey in 1985. I am sure that the larger and more successful companies will appear in Value Line by the late 1980s, but until then, the most essential source of information and evaluation is unavailable. But second, it seems that these stocks, as a group, are so richly priced that much of their rosy future is discounted. Genentech, for example, has often traded at 50–100 times its current earnings, so that even were it reviewed by Value Line, its minimum 3–5 year appreciation potential might not exceed 100 percent.* Disenchantment with the profit growth prospects for these companies will invariably set in, and this may provide an opportunity for a patient and disciplined investor to participate in the biotechnological revolution.

There are, in fact, several firms regularly reviewed by Value Line which do spend 7.5 percent of sales on research and development, but are not reviewed in the electronics, computer, or precision instrument industry groups. In a few cases, such as John Fluke Manufacturing, they probably should be, based on the Value Line business description. Fluke provides equipment for the semiconductor industry, and I would not rule it out simply because Value Line may have misclassified the company. On the other hand, there are firms in the drug industry, for example, which may spend 7.5 percent or more on research and development. I have excluded them from consideration in the PAD system in order to concentrate on those companies in the forefront of the technological revolution. But, as I pointed out in Chapter 8, an investor with less faith in the revolution, or a greater need for diversification and security, can modify the rules of Chapters 2–4 only slightly and build a much more diversified portfolio. Stocks of firms such as the drug companies, which spend relatively heavily on R&D, may be ideal candidates for this expanded PAD portfolio, since the 7.5 percent R&D rule would not have to be substantially relaxed in these cases.

E. COMPUTERS AND INVESTING

The information revolution is changing the way we invest. Computers have made it possible for the New York Stock Exchange (NYSE) and its member firms to manage volume in excess of 200,000,000 shares per day. Computers enable the NASD's NASDAQ system to trade over 100,000,000

---

*Genentech is now reviewed by Value Line.

shares in a single day without a central trading floor or face-to-face trading. These numbers are truly astounding when we recall that average daily trading volume on the NYSE was 5,000,000 shares at the beginning of the 1960s. Information on trading is transmitted instantaneously around the world, and individual investors can purchase portable hand-held computer/receivers that can provide up-to-the-second quotations on thousands of stocks, futures, and options contracts. A personal computer owner can review the same information over telephone lines or via FM broadcast signals. These technological marvels are not of direct interest to the PAD investor, however, since trading is relatively infrequent with the PAD system, and up-to-the-second quotations are unnecessary. Even the eventual linkup of exchanges around the world, permitting around-the-clock trading, would have little impact on the PAD investor. I suppose if you had made up your mind to buy or sell a stock today, and then the press of work or other activity caused you to forget until after 4 p.m. Eastern Time, it would be useful to be able to call your broker after dinner and have your transaction carried out that evening in Tokyo or Hong Kong. Waiting until the next day would not be that painful or costly in most situations, however.

The computer revolution has also made it possible to bypass the human side of your brokerage firm altogether, entering your buy or sell orders via computer and telephone line. It certainly does not pay to purchase a computer, modem, and accessories just to partake of this service, but I admit that surly or uncooperative stockbrokers can drive an investor to prefer the quiet neutrality of a green-screen computer monitor. Others may prefer the human touch. To each his own.

Portfolio analysis is also simplified by the computer. A wide variety of software is available to help you keep track of your transactions, dividends, and portfolio value. I find these programs about as useful as checkbook balancing programs. It is still easier for all but the most arithmetically retarded to use a checkbook register and an old-fashioned word processor (a pencil or pen).

One program that does deserve special mention is Value/Screen, a product of Value Line. Value/Screen software enables the user to select stocks from the Value Line universe using criteria similar to those laid out in Chapters 2 and 3. It also contains a portfolio information module, which lets you store key information about your portfolio. While this product could automate much of the PAD system, it has several drawbacks, namely, it is only available monthly, and the "screens" do not match up with the precise rules of Chapters 2 and 3. For example, it is impossible to select stocks based on R&D percentage or on the basis of appreciation potential to the low end of the 3–5 year range. Nonetheless, this program is the forerunner of more flexible software that will appear in the future. Once a PAD investor can "interrogate" the complete Value Line database with a computer, the time that must be devoted to stock-screening elements of the PAD system can be reduced to minutes per week.

F. MANAGING THE INFORMATION FLOW

Until the computer revolution is complete, however, PAD investors must deal with a significant burden of paper. In the following sections I give suggestions that can keep the paper flowing smoothly, with a minimum of confusion. Once a household robot can do these chores, as well as serve drinks and ward off intruders, buy it.

1. Recordkeeping

If you are ever audited by the IRS, you will quickly discover that you are at a major disadvantage without good records. Good recordkeeping will also help you in preparing your annual Schedule D, "Capital Gains and Losses," with a minimum of pain and suffering. Accordingly, keep a record of every transaction you make. Your discount broker will provide you with an extra copy in addition to the remittance copy for every transaction. Keep a stock record book of some kind (purchase price may be tax-deductible), in which you can list your holdings, dates of purchases and sales, amounts of profits and losses, and dividends. One inexpensive loose-leaf book that will do this for you is listed at the end of this chapter. If you record your transactions as you make them, with a separate listing of short- and long-term gains and losses for the year, you can see at a glance what your tax situation is in August. Also, when tax time arrives, you (or your preparer) can copy your entries directly onto Schedule D.

One additional piece of information you will want to keep for every stock you own is the name and address of the transfer agent for the common stock. Banks usually handle this work, and every stock certificate has the name of the transfer agent on it. Corporate annual reports also contain this information. If your securities are ever lost or stolen, you must contact the transfer agent. The transfer agent will want to know the serial numbers on your certificates, so you should write down these numbers also. Keep your securities in a safe place (see below), since replacing them can be a lengthy and expensive process.

If you keep your certificates and maintain your records as I have suggested, you can then use the "identified cost" method for calculating your taxable gains and losses. This method is more flexible than either the "first-in, first-out" (FIFO) or "last-in, first-out" (LIFO) methods of accounting. The identified cost method makes it much easier to postpone gains when that is advantageous and to convert short-term gains to long-term. To use the method, every purchase and sale must be "identified" with stock certificate numbers. Then, when it is time to sell some stock, you can select which block or blocks of shares to sell based on purchase date and price. Here is an example.

Suppose you bought 100 shares of stock X at 38 on May 6, 1982, another 100 at 35 on September 8, 1982, and a final 100 at 40 on November 10, 1982. Suppose also that by April 1983 the stock market has risen sharply and it is time to sell some stock. Stock X, at 83, is one of those you decide to sell. If the holding period for long-term capital gains is one year, any of the shares you sell will be taxed at the short-term rate, since you have not held any shares for a year. To minimize the tax paid, you can sell the shares bought at 40, on which you have the smallest gain. This minimizes your tax now and leaves more of your gains to be taxed at long-term rates. If the stock had declined instead, the sale of the stock at 40 would provide the largest tax loss. While in this case LIFO accounting would provide the same result, the next sale under LIFO would be the stock bought at 35, whereas with identified cost, you could sell the stock bought at 38 next if you wished. If you know that your tax bracket in the current year will be either much higher or much lower than the following year, you can use the identified cost method to push more taxable income into the lower tax rate year. In the example here, suppose also that this year is a low-tax year for you. You might then want to sell the 100 shares bought at 35 instead, so that the biggest gain is taxed at the lower rate. If the holding period for long-term capital gains were six months instead, you would want to sell the first shares you purchased. LIFO accounting would force you to sell the one block of shares that would not qualify for favorable tax treatment.

This flexibility of the identified cost method does require extra record-keeping, but it is well worth it. Note also that in this example we have stuck to the advice of Section A: our tax strategy has not dictated our portfolio strategy!

2. Safekeeping of Securities

The identified cost method is simpler if you take possession of your securities. Even if you do not want or need to use this method, I still recommend that you take possession of your securities rather than leave the certificates on deposit with your broker. If you have your securities on deposit, your broker will mail them to you at your request. Brokerage houses do fail, and when they do, customer balances and securities can be tied up for long periods of time, even though customers are insured by the Securities Investor Protection Corporation (SIPC). Do not keep your securities at home. They will be safer in a safe deposit box at your local bank, and the small fee for the box is often tax deductible. Selling your stock will now entail a trip to the bank and a visit to your safe deposit box, and the mailing of the certificates to the broker. This extra time and effort raises the "cost" of trading in and out of the market and thus may help make you a patient investor. In addition, placing your securities in a bank vault may create an aura of permanence, which will militate against short-term trading. The risk that your securities will be stolen in the mails is minimal if you mail them unendorsed at the same time that you mail a "stock power" form to the broker separately. Your broker can instruct you on even simpler endorsement procedures, which will also keep the risk of theft to a minimum.

3. Where to Keep Your Cash Reserves

Where should you keep your funds awaiting reinvestment? I would not leave them on deposit with your broker, because I believe this creates a subtle pressure to reinvest them. I recommend a money market mutual fund (MMMF) with free check-writing privileges and low fees for wiring money. It is quite simple to deposit money in an MMMF, and it is just as simple to write a check against your MMMF balance to pay for stock purchases. There are many good-quality funds with the features I have mentioned, and there are services that rate the safety of funds if you are in doubt. Whenever possible, I limit myself to those which invest in Treasury securities only, or those which are insured by an insurance company. The yield is lower in these cases, but the loss of a fraction of a percent is well worth the extra security for me. For this reason I would pay no attention to the comparative yields listed in the newspaper, since the differences are often too small to be significant and they may reflect different degrees of risk. For example, some MMMFs buy commercial paper, which usually has a higher yield than many other short-term instruments. But commercial paper is an unsecured IOU. When Penn Central failed in 1970, holders of their commercial paper lost their entire investment.

PAD investors in high tax brackets can keep their cash reserves in a (federal) tax-free fund investing in short-term municipal obligations. Many of the major fund groups offer this type of investment. In some cases the interest could also be exempt from state and local taxes.

4. Mail

The other kind of paper that can overwhelm you is provided free by the companies in your portfolio. Every year you will receive quarterly reports, and an annual report and proxy statement from each company in which you own shares. If the firm pays dividends, you may also receive four separate dividend checks. Additional materials may appear in your mailbox regularly: a report on the annual meeting, for example, or press releases, or, when a proxy fight or takeover battle is looming, seemingly endless missives from the antagonists. If you have always felt that you never received enough mail, investing can help solve your problem. If you already spend as much time with your mail as you like, I have a few time-saving suggestions.

First, remember that corporate reports are essentially self-serving and that all of the information has been disseminated on Wall Street by the time you read it. Remember also that your proxy means very little, since, in the Russian style, you can only vote for the nominees or withhold your vote, with few exceptions. If the firm is performing in accordance with expectations, I routinely sign and mail the proxy card. I would not bother to vote against any proposal that management favored, unless it would make the company a difficult takeover target. Since most takeovers tend to benefit stockholders, I do not like to see them made too difficult. I ignore the proxy statement itself unless it contains some of these anti-takeover provisions. The annual report, which often comes in the same package, is much more pleasant to read, although it is often filled with self-congratulatory kudos in good years and pious platitudes in bad. (High-technology companies, however, are more likely to have pictures of new technology which are fun to look at.) *Never* make a buy or sell decision about a company based on the annual report. Although I keep the most recent annual report of each company whose shares I own, my pile of reports gathers dust. A PAD investor can safely throw them away, along with the quarterly reports. It can be dangerous to know your companies too well, since objectivity is quickly lost.

If you want to study the numbers in detail beyond the level of Value Line, write for the company's 10-K report if it is not included with the annual report. The address to write to is normally listed at the end of the annual report. The 10-K has more detail and no fluff. One feature of the 10-K that can be valuable to a PAD investor is the section on business competition. The stock of the chief competitor of your company may also be a good investment!

5. Watching Your Stocks and the Market

PAD techniques do not require a large amount of time. Review of the *Value Line Investment Survey* should only take an hour a week, and daily review of the *Wall Street Journal* should take two hours a week or less. Reading the Sunday *New York Times* Business section can give you a flavor of market action for the week just passed, as will "Wall Street Week" on Friday night, when the latest reading of the Technical Market Index is revealed. The only additional required time is for occasional quiet contemplation of the market's condition and direction, and the performance of your portfolio. I recommend that this time be spent on weekends, when your pace of life can be a little more relaxed.

It is possible, however, to spend all your waking hours reading financial publications, watching Financial News Network, the "Nightly Business Report," and other financial programs. I cannot recommend any of these to anyone without a will of iron, because it is so tempting to listen to the siren song of one market expert or another who says "Buy this" or "Sell that." A Patient and Disciplined investor must limit exposure to prevailing market wisdom.

There is also no reason to call your broker for quotes on the market or your individual stocks. This practice wastes your valuable time. It is akin to social drinking by reformed alcoholics. It is dangerous.

6. Updating the PAD System

No stock market system can or should be immutable for all time. The PAD System has evolved over many years, and it will continue to do so. If you wish to be informed of the current status of the PAD System please write to the "PAD System Report," P.O. Box 554, Oxford, OH 45056.

G. PAD NO-NO'S: SELLING SHORT, COMMODITY FUTURES, AND PONZI SCHEMES

1. Selling Short

You can sell a stock that you do not own. And you can borrow from your broker half of the collateral you need to do it. If the stock falls in price, you can repurchase it, which is called covering, and your profit is the difference between your sale and purchase prices, minus commissions and interest paid. I think it would be an error for a PAD investor to sell short. The PAD system is designed for long-term capital gains. When the great bull market of the eighties and nineties is in full swing, a PAD investor should not be betting on market declines. If the market becomes overvalued as described in Chapter 4, initiate a selling program. Eventually, if you are skillful and lucky, the market will take all your stock off your hands at extravagant prices. Then stay liquid. Extreme greed could drive stocks to levels beyond all reason, and if you are caught short, you will start giving back your hard-earned profits. There is certainly good money to be made on the short side of the market, but you can't learn how to do it with the PAD system.

2. Commodity Futures

Don't do it. If you don't want to take my word for it, here is the opinion of a professional futures trader as reported in *The Traders* (p. 143) by Sonny Kleinfeld (see Readings section):

> Over a late lunch, Stone tells me that the public probably shouldn't fool around with futures. He imparts this advice even though professional traders derive a good chunk of their profits from dull-witted trading by Mr. Average Investor. To the professional, members of the public are looked on as lambs available for fleecing.

3. The Ponzi Scheme

Every year investors are bilked out of millions of dollars by clever con men who use variations on the Ponzi scheme. Ponzi himself produced phenomenal gains for his first investors, and money poured in as the stories of sudden fabulous gains spread. Unfortunately, the gains to the first investors were financed by the payments of the latecomers. Ponzi's scheme and all others like it end when the supply of fools no longer can grow fast enough to finance the growing number of existing players. Always assume you are a latecomer to these deals that seem to be too good to be true. They probably are.

Readings for the PAD Investor

J.K. Lasser's Stock Record Book. Published by Chartcraft/Investor's Intelligence, 1 West Avenue, Larchmont, NY 10538. A cheap ($10.00), easy-to-use loose-leaf binder to record all your stock transactions and related data. I use it.

The *Wall Street Journal.* Published by Dow-Jones and Co., 200 Liberty St., New York, NY 10281. The *Journal* has just about all the tax information you will ever need.

SONNY KLEINFELD, *The Traders.* New York: Holt, Rinehart and Winston, 1984. Watch the little porkers end up in the supermarket.

JOHN G. SIMON, *The Ethical Investor.* New Haven: Yale University Press, 1972. The classic in the field.

11

CONCLUSIONS

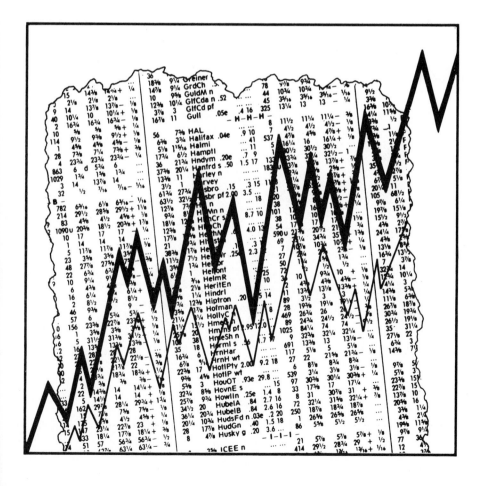

"Good things come to those who wait."

You are now ready to start a new life as a PAD investor. Before you jump in with both feet, however, I want to review briefly the elements of the PAD system for outperforming Wall Street. First and foremost, you must follow the rules. These rules, which have evolved over many years of experience, will keep you from running with the pack. This instinct, which we have all inherited, had survival value eons ago. But on Wall Street today the herd instinct will lead you to ruin. The PAD rules will also overcome the desire for a quick profit, which, if unchecked, will soon have you running with the pack again. As I argued in Chapter 7, it is almost impossible to beat the market except over the long term, and the PAD system is a long-term system.

The rules of Chapters 2 and 3 will help you select growth stocks that have the potential to double or triple. These rules will also force you to hold those stocks patiently. The rules of Chapter 4 will improve your market timing, so that your buying of growth stocks is more likely to coincide with periods of pessimism and good value, and your selling of them is more likely to coincide with periods of optimism and excessive valuations.

If you buy PAD stocks at market tops and sell them at market bottoms, you will not profit from the PAD system.

Many systems have little to say about selling. The PAD rules will help you sell winners, forcing you to lighten up rather than hold forever, and sell losers, because there is a time to give up and look elsewhere. You must be prepared to take losses.

If you follow these rules and limit yourself to the universe of Value Line stocks, you may be able to resist the temptation to buy the local startup firm on which you just got a hot tip from your uncle's brother-in-law. Value Line is so much a part of my investment routine that I could not imagine buying any stock without having read the Value Line report first!

The only other rules are in Chapter 8. Conservative investors and aggressive investors can also use the modified rules of Chapter 8 to improve their investment performance. The first section of Chapter 8 will also come in handy for a PAD investor who is starting out with a non-PAD portfolio and wishes to gradually convert to a PAD portfolio. The non-PAD stocks can be managed with the rules of this chapter.

I believe it would be a mistake to ignore the other chapters of the book, however. Without some understanding of the vicissitudes of the economy and economic policy, you will be at the mercy of monetarists, gold bugs, and other strange creatures who may convince you that the sky is falling. A strong dose of Chapter 5 can keep you from turning into Chicken Little. J. M. Keynes, an economist who understood financial markets, said it best: "Practical men, who believe themselves to be quite exempt from any intellectual influences, are usually the slaves of some defunct economist."* Chapter 5 will also help you cast a discerning eye on the Federal Reserve, the money numbers, and the budget, to determine whether the economy is headed for rough sailing before reaching the Valhalla of the electronic revolution. A little economics goes a long way.

If you have accepted the PAD system wholeheartedly, you have accepted my vision of the future outlined in Chapter 6. My vision of the future could be wrong. No one has a good record of predicting the future in any detail. If you disagree with my rosy scenario, then Chapter 8 can help you apply the PAD system to a non-PAD portfolio. But if my vision of a benign electronic revolution is right, many PAD stocks have a very bright future. Indeed, as the future unfolds, Chapter 6 can help you spot the new and important trends in the ongoing electronic revolution. Entire

---

The General Theory of Employment, Interest, and Money London: (MacMillan, 1936), p. 383.

new industries may spring up that we cannot imagine in the 1980s. You will have to decide whether they are PAD industries for the 1990s. (On the other hand, if you are even more of a technological optimist than me, use the second part of Chapter 8 to guide you in the financial "fast-lane." Remember, though, that crashes are often fatal at high speeds!)

Readers who foundered in Chapter 9 are forgiven. An experienced PAD investor with a substantial portfolio should review Chapter 9 carefully, however. Large portfolios can be "insured" cheaply with Standard and Poor's options strategies. The small or inexperienced PAD investor can save Chapter 9 until his or her portfolio has reached the requisite size.

I am fully aware that many readers will but scan Chapter 7. It provides no advice for making money. But it is a very important chapter: not only does it explain why a book like this can provide superior returns for readers, but it also shows how the PAD system is grounded in the same economic theories which are slowly undermining the notion of "efficient markets." John Maynard Keynes knew that markets were not efficient in 1936. I am sure he would endorse the arguments of Chapter 7, since they echo Chapter 12 of his monumental *General Theory of Employment, Interest, and Money*. Even though past performance is no guarantee of future success, there is good reason to believe that the PAD system will continue to work in the future as well as it has in the past.

A. FINAL WORDS OF ADVICE (FOR THE SKEPTIC)

It took me many years and many mistakes to develop the PAD system to its present form. It thus took me many years to become a full-fledged PAD investor. If you also prefer the gradual approach, start with the PAD system on a "trial" basis. Start with the following three rules:

1. Don't buy stock when Chapter 4 says sell.
2. Don't sell stock when Chapter 4 says buy.
3. Use Value Line (and only Value Line) to build and monitor your portfolio.

These three rules alone can turn an average investor into a superior investor. If it happens to you, try the whole system. And good luck to you!

EPILOGUE

Although *Outperforming Wall Street* does not come with a warranty, the PAD System should provide many years of trouble-free operation. It will work in bull markets and bear markets, helping you pick good growth stocks when the market is cheap and then forcing you to hold them until the market is dear. Value Line is the only external source of information required.

The purpose of this epilogue is to clarify several minor points, on a variety of topics, in light of events too recent to be included in the preceding chapters of this book. For ease of exposition, I have arranged my commentaries by issues rather than chapters.

Tax Reform.　In August 1986, it became a near certainty that major tax revision would be signed into law by President Reagan. How much of the revision is true "reform" is debatable. There will be billions of dollars allocated to "transition rules" which are thinly disguised tax breaks for the few and powerful. Many other tax breaks will be preserved under the new law. Nonetheless, using the criteria of Chapter 10, the new law is on balance true tax reform. Americans should rightly perceive the new system as fairer than the old system, since many of the most abusive tax shelters will be curtailed or eliminated, and poor taxpayers will be removed from the rolls altogether. At the same time, stiff minimum tax calculations will make it more difficult for the wealthy to avoid paying taxes. If Americans are convinced that the system is fairer, perhaps voluntary compliance will increase.

Several changes affect PAD investors directly. Capital gains will now be taxed at ordinary income rates. The maximum will thus be 28 percent compared to the former 20 percent. This change is relatively minor, especially for long-term investors. My only quibble is that the capital gains tax should apply to real, inflation-adjusted gains instead of nominal gains. We already index the system for wage-earners. In spite of this change, there is still no reason to let tax strategy dominate investment strategy.

Some investors will see their capital gains tax rates increase by a more substantial amount under the new system. A taxpayer in the 35 percent bracket under the old system paid 14 percent tax on long-term capital gains (.35 × .4). This taxpayer will probably fall in the 28 percent bracket under the new system, paying twice as high a tax rate on capital gains. Many of these investors with capital gains will want to realize them in 1986 rather than 1987. Since most investors, unlike PAD investors (see Chapter 10), do their tax-selling at the very end of the year, there could be a brief, but severe, downdraft in the market at the end of 1986. The best-performing stocks of 1986 may lead the way down, since they are the ones that are most likely to have generated gains.

Many conservative PAD investors (see Chapter 8) will reap a windfall under the new tax system, since the rate at which their dividend income is taxed will fall. Income stocks were bid up sharply in the summer of 1986 in anticipation of this higher after-tax return. However, PAD investors should not jump on the Wall Street bandwagon and forsake growth stocks. Growth stocks still have the advantage of historically high average returns over long periods of time, and they still provide the tax-deferral features of "inside buildup."

Corporate taxes will rise on balance under the new system. The reduction in the top corporate rate will be offset by the retroactive elimination of the Investment Tax Credit and by less generous depreciation schedules, and many other changes. As I noted in Chapter 10, it is best to let Value Line factor all the changes into its estimates of future earnings. This process should be completed by November 1986, and all the rules of Chapters

2–4 will still apply. *There is no need to alter the PAD system.* Some PAD companies will probably pay less in taxes under the new system.

No one knows what the net economic impact of the new tax system will be. Some have argued that economic growth will be speeded up, others that it will be impaired. We can only hope that sensible fiscal and monetary policy will offset any adverse consequences. Also, it is quite likely that there will be more changes made in our tax system in 1987, 1988, and beyond. Major errors can be corrected.

The Deficit.   Sensible fiscal policy may be a contradiction in terms with Gramm-Rudman. Although we may avoid massive budget cuts in the 1987 fiscal year, the arbitrary targets for the deficit in the following years will be extremely difficult to reach. As I discussed in Chapters 5 and 6, balancing the budget is not always good fiscal policy, especially in recession, and balancing the budget with massive across-the-board cuts is politically unacceptable and economically unwise. I doubt we can grow our way out of the deficits. The only remaining sensible alternative is to selectively reduce spending, sparing no sacred cows, and increase taxes, calling them "user fees" if that fig leaf is necessary. (Of course I do not have to run for reelection.) Gramm-Rudman may provide the necessary crisis which will force Congress and the White House to undertake the sensible alternatives.

The deficit should be reduced, so that monetary policy can continue to be accomodative. This should help keep the dollar in a gradual descent. This, in turn, will eventually lead to an improvement in our stubborn trade deficit, allowing us to reduce our worrisome dependence on foreign capital inflows.

Monetary Policy.   Someday Paul Volcker will step down as Chairman of the Federal Reserve Board of Governors. It will not be a happy day for the financial markets, although there was life before "Saint Paul." Until that time, the Federal Reserve will be as accommodative as possible without rekindling inflation. Rapid growth of M1 has clearly not rekindled inflation. A bitter pill for the monetarists.

The Dollar and the Trade Deficit.   The falling dollar should start reducing our trade deficit by the end of 1986. It often takes more than a year for trade flows to be substantially altered in response to exchange rate changes. In addition, the dollar has not fallen against the currencies of some of our biggest trading partners (e.g. Canada). The trade deficit has spurred rising protectionist sentiment in the United States. Although the Congress did not override the President's 1986 veto of a grossly protectionist trade bill, the vote was extremely close. Our only hope is that a shrinking trade deficit will stop the slide down the protectionist slope.

The Bull Market.   August 1986 marked the fourth birthday of the Wall Street bull market. While it is not at all unlikely that the Dow will climb to the 3000 level before the end of the decade, there will certainly be major stumbles along the way. The speculative excesses which will have appeared in full force by the time we reach 3000 almost guarantee that a nasty bear market will follow. Even at Dow 1900, the bull is beginning to show signs of age. Review Chapter 4 carefully before you invest.

PAD Stocks.   The 1986 leg of the bull market has not been kind to some of my favorite PAD Stocks. Advanced Micro and Intel have been especially weak, reflecting poor short-term prospects for the semiconductor industry. New PAD investors applying the rules of Chapter 2 will avoid these stocks until their Value Line rankings improve. On the other hand, Amdahl, Cray Research, Digital Equipment, and Tandem Computers have done quite well, but their 3–5 year appreciation potentials are much less enticing than they were in the fall of 1985. While many special situation stocks are quite cheap (see Chapter 8), these are very risky and volatile shares.

Patience and Discipline.   A system based on patience and discipline will not provide instant results for new converts. Many months, and perhaps years, of the PAD regimen may be necessary before its full fruits are realized. "The secret of success is constancy to purpose."

LISTING OF
ALL RULES

CHAPTER TWO

1. Appreciation potential must be at least 100 percent to the low end of the range.
2. Estimated future earnings must be at least 100 percent higher than earnings of the most recently completed year (or the estimate for the year in progress).
3. A financial strength rating below "B" or a safety rating of "5" (lowest) disqualifies the company.
4. R&D percentage must be at least 7.5 percent.
5. Short-term performance ranking must be higher than "5" (lowest).
6. Diversify!

CHAPTER THREE

Buying

1. Use a discount broker exclusively.

2. Buy stocks on your Buy List at fixed intervals.
3. Do not buy on margin.
4. Use market orders only.

Selling

1. Sell between one-fourth and one-half of your holding when it has tripled, and then sell additional fractions if it rises substantially more. (Use stock splits to ease the pain of parting.)
2. If a stock has declined 50 percent from purchase price, or has performed significantly worse than the market for six months, or has dropped to a "5" for short-term performance, it must be reevaluated carefully.
3. If a stock reviewed under Rule 2 survives a reevaluation, cash reserves can be committed to it. If the price has fallen, this will enable you to "average down." This rule should be invoked only once for any stock and does not apply to a short-term "5."
4. Do not use stoploss orders.
5. Use market orders only.
6. Sell when a merger or buyout is announced.
7. Review every stock in your portfolio at least once every three months.
8. Sell stocks on your Sell List at fixed intervals.

CHAPTER FOUR

1. The market is OK to buy if Value Line Investment Survey Median Appreciation Potential equals or exceeds 100 percent. Selling should be undertaken when this potential is below 75 percent. 75–95 percent is a neutral area.
2. Do not commence a buying program under Rule 1 if the "Wall Street Week" Technical Market Index has a sell signal in effect.

CHAPTER EIGHT

Conservative

1C. Average annual total return must be at least 19 percent to the low end of the range.

2C. Estimated future earnings must be at least 50 percent higher than earnings of the best year of the last five years (including the year in progress).

3C. A financial strength rating below "B⁺⁺" or a safety rating below "3" (average) disqualifies the company.

4C. R&D percentage must be at least 2 percent.

5C. Short-term performance ranking must be higher than "4" (below average).

Aggressive

1S. A special situation must be rated at least a "buy/hold."

2S. A special situation must have a 3–5 year appreciation potential of at least 200 percent.

3S. Purchase one-half of your eventual investment when Rules 1S and 2S are satisfied. Then wait at least three months before completing your investment.

4S. Do not purchase additional shares more than once.

5S. Sell all of your holdings of a stock that is rated "switch" by Value Line.

6S. Sell one-fourth to one-half of your holding when the stock has tripled in price.

7S. Sell additional fractions of your holdings at higher multiples of your cost.

8S. Select stocks rated "hold" with low appreciation potential for your Sell List.

9S. Maintain your specials portfolio at a maximum of 25 percent of your total PAD portfolio.

10S. Do not "churn" your specials portfolio.

11S. Diversify your portfolio.

INDEX